IN SEARCH
OF TRUE
WISDOM

SERGIUS BOLSHAKOFF AND
M. BASIL PENNINGTON, OCSO

IN SEARCH
OF TRUE
WISDOM

Visits to Eastern Spiritual Fathers

ALBA · HOUSE   NEW · YORK

SOCIETY OF ST. PAUL, 2187 VICTORY BLVD., STATEN ISLAND, NEW YORK 10314

"Conference of Archimandrite Sophrony" originally appeared, under the title "The Monks of Mt. Athos," in *Monastic Exchange*, Summer 1977, Vol. 9, No. 2.

"Archimandrite Sophrony: Disciple of Father Silouan" originally appeared, under the title "A Spiritual Father: Archimandrite Sophrony," In *Monastic Exchange*, Autumn 1972, Vol. 4, No. 3.

"A Noble Spiritual Mother: Mother Alexandra" originally appeared in *Monastic Exchange*, Fall 1978, Vol. 10, No. 3.

"Mount Athos in Boston: Archimandrite Panteleimon" originally appeared in *Diakonia*, 1978, Vol. 13, No. 3.

Library of Congress Cataloging-in-Publication Data

Bolshakoff, Serge.
    In Search of true wisdom : visits to Eastern spiritual fathers / Sergius Bolshakoff and M. Basil Pennington.
    Reprint. Originally published: Garden City, N.Y. : Doubleday, 1979.
       p.   cm.
    ISBN 0-8189-0616-2
    1. Monastic and religious life. 2. Monasticism and religious orders, Orthodox Eastern. 3. Spirituality — Orthodox Eastern Church. 4. Orthodox Eastern Church — Doctrines. 5. Bolshakoff, Serge. 6. Pennington, M. Basil. 7. Monks — Interviews. 8. Nuns — Interviews. I. Pennington, M. Basil. II. Title.
BX581.B64 1991   91-17585
271'.8 — dc20   CIP

Designed, printed and bound in the United States of America by the Fathers and Brothers of the Society of St. Paul, 2187 Victory Boulevard, Staten Island, New York 10314, as part of their communications apostolate.

PRINTING INFORMATION:

Current Printing - first digit 1 2 3 4 5 6 7 8 9 10 11 12

Year of Current Printing - first year shown
1991   1992   1993   1994   1995   1996   1997   1998

PREFACE

I had arrived at the Cistercian Abbey of Scourment, a stone's throw from the French-Belgian border, late on a winter day. Darkness had set in, and the monks were already in choir chanting the evening office. So I slipped into the visitor's gallery adjoining the guesthouse. When the last, graceful echoes had blended into the silent climate of prayer, I quietly rose and started toward the guesthouse. At the door, I met him. No introductions were necessary. We had corresponded for years, and though we had no expectations of meeting at this time or in this place, I knew immediately that the elderly gentleman who graciously bowed me through the door was Dr. Sergius Bolshakoff. We embraced as Russian Christians do and then repaired to his room to enjoy an evening of sharing and presence. Out of that evening comes this volume.

By the time of our meeting, Dr. Bolshakoff was well known to monks of the West. More times than he could count, he had been a guest in our monasteries from one end of Europe to the other, and beyond, during his fifty years and more as a pilgrim of ecumenism.

His unending journey had begun in 1919, when the aftermath of the revolution forced the devout young man, who wanted nothing to do with service in the godless army of the Bolsheviks, to emigrate from his native land. He had settled in Estonia and was seeking to complete his education as an engineer when, one day, he read a curious item in the Russian newspaper from Paris. The papal nuncio, Monsignor Alexander Evreinov, had celebrated Liturgy according to the Synodal rite for the Russian Catholics in the capital. Intrigued by this, Bolshakoff contacted the local Catholic pastor to obtain some information about Russian Catholics and their communities outside Russia.

He conceived a great desire to work for the unity of these Russian Christians in the face of the common godless enemy. Advice seemed to indicate he must first get steeped in his own Orthodoxy, and so he began to pursue theological studies at Pskovo-Petchersky Monastery. It was the needs of this monastery, especially in face of its efforts to establish a true seminary, that first sent the young theologian to the West, to the newly established Latin-Byzantine Benedictine Monastery at Amay — today's Chevtogne. His experience there was a good one, greatly enriched by almost daily contact with Dom Lambert Beauduin. At the end of the visit, when he sought to return, he found the borders of Estonia closed to him. The poor country had all the penniless Russian refugees it could afford. And thus began the homeless exile's peregrinations.

Over the course of the next two years, Bolshakoff became convinced not only that his life must be spent in the cause of Church unity but that one of the most effective ways to work toward it was by simple presence. Christians of East and West, especially monks, needed to share in each other's community life and search for God, the source of all unity. In England, on December 27, 1928, in the Anglican Benedictine Monastery of Nashdown, established in the former manor house of the Russian Prince Alexis Dolgoruki, Sergius Bolshakoff made a lifetime commitment. In the hands of the Orthodox Bishop of Berlin, Tikhon Ljoshenko, whom he had served as secretary, he promised to seek perfection according to the Rule of Saint Benedict as a lay oblate and to work for Christian unity.

Besides its extraordinary context, this profession had particular significance since it was the first time an Orthodox had committed himself to the Rule of the Patriarch of Western monasticism since the Benedictine monasteries on Mount Athos* died out, in the thirteenth century.

---

* *Note: At the end of the volume there is a Glossary of those expressions common to the Russian monastic milieu that occur in these texts but might not be familiar to the average Western reader. The first time each of these appears, it is marked with an asterisk.*

Saint Benedict has always been held in great honor among Eastern Christians. His life, written by Pope Saint Gregory the Great — called in the East the *Dialogos* because of the *Dialogues* in which he recounts the lives of Saint Benedict and other Italian saints — is well known. Saint Joseph of Vokolamsk drew heavily upon him when he wrote the last great Russian monastic rule, at the beginning of the sixteenth century. At least three verbal citation from Saint Benedict's Rule are found in the primitive Typicon,* or Constitution, of Mount Athos, drawn up by Saint Athanasios, the founder of the Great Lavra Monastery. Saint Theophan the Recluse, a great Russian mystic of the nineteenth century, translated Saint Benedict's Rule into Russian.

In the course of the following decades, Brother Sergius moved about from monastery to monastery, spending anywhere from a week to nearly a year with Benedictine and Cistercian communities in all parts of Europe. Elsewhere he has published candid and colorful accounts of many of these visits. When the Second World War placed restrictions on his movements, he industriously employed the time to obtain his degree as Doctor of Philosophy at Christ Church, Oxford, publishing his thesis, "The Doctrine of the Unity of the Church in the Works of Khomyakon and Moehler," in 1946. But throughout these decades Bolshakoff was concerned about growing ever deeper in his own Russian Orthodox tradition and spirituality. It was for this reason he seized whatever opportunities offered themselves to visit the great Spiritual Fathers who still lived among the Russian monks in exile, and on one occasion even returned to Russia itself. From the Fathers, he received the teaching that served as the basis for his own spiritual life. And it is something of this rich traditional spiritual teaching that he shares with us in the narratives that follow.

I have taken the liberty to add a few accounts of my own, the last five in the volume. They relate visits that are quite recent and therefore much of a generation after the visits of Brother Sergius. They give witness to the fact that not only on Mount Athos and in Greece but even in England and America the rich spiritual traditions that had so enlivened Russian Christian life in the decades preceding the godless revolution still live on. I have added to these narratives translations of conferences by some of these great Spiritual Fathers and Mothers which I think convey far more fully and eloquently the richness, depth, and beauty of their spiritual teaching.

An extensive synthesis of the teaching to be found in this volume seems uncalled for here. The best introduction would be Dr. Bolshakoff's earlier volume *Russian Mystics*, with its Foreword by the late Thomas Merton. The Fathers and Mother who speak here speak out of that deep, rich spiritual tradition that found a most life-giving soil in the vastness of Russia, with its endless solitudes and its hearty peasantry. They were a people close to the reality of God's Providence, who had the simplicity of life and leisure to let it pervade and inform the whole of their lives.

The first nursery of this spirituality was the same as that which served the West: the deceptively barren wastes of Egypt. As this spirituality began to be articulated, Saint John Cassian, whom Eastern Christians refer to as "the Roman," brought one very pervasive and influential expression of it to the West. It flourished and retained much of its pristine purity right up to the eve of the Protestant Reformation. The justly famous anonymous work, still very widely read, *The Cloud of Unknowing* is a witness to this. An eloquent testimony to the fact that this work and the tradition it gave expression to remained exquisitely faithful to their origins is the fact that the late Bishop of Corinth, in his introduction to a recent Greek translation of *The Cloud of Unknowing*, did not hesitate to declare it to be the work of an unknown fourteenth-century English *Orthodox* writer. The contemplative and mystical tradition suffered virtual shipwreck in the West in the sixteenth century for reasons that Abbot Thomas Keating recently expounded with great clarity in the book *Finding Grace at the Center*. As the Western Christian community, in the wake of the Second Vatican Council, looked to its sources and sought to recover the contemplative dimension of its life, this tradition received a new, somewhat modernized though very faithful expression in what has come to be called Centering Prayer.

One of the most insightful exponents of this early spirituality, Evagrius Ponticus, fell under a cloud of suspicion because some Origenist heresies crept into his dogmatic works and brought about his condemnation. But his articulation of the spiritual was of such richness that it could not be lost, and found its way back into the life-giving currents of the tradition under the name of the venerated Russian mystic Saint Nilos.

The simple tradition of the Fathers of the Desert, as it passed on through successive generations of monks in the East, was enriched or added to, at times by sources from outside Christianity. One has only to compare the rather complex psychosomatic method of the Jesus Prayer, presented by the great teachers of hesychasm* in the fourteenth century, Nicephorus and Gregory of Sinai, with the *dhikr* prayer of the Sufis in the thirteenth century and the *nembutsu* practices of the Buddhists in Japan in the twelfth, to have ample indication of this. But the tradition that flourished in Russia and in the Rossikon* and the many Russian sketes* on Mount Athos remained essentially simple and pure. One reading Father Silouan, who died at the Rossikon in 1938, and hearing of his practice can easily identify it with that of Abba Isaac in fourth-century Egypt as well as with today's current Western form of Centering Prayer. It was with this pure tradition that Dr. Bolshakoff was constantly in touch as he visited the last of the Russian Startzy.*

In the West today, thanks to many fine publication projects, we can easily get in touch with not only the ancient witnesses of this tradition such as the great hesychasts* in the *Philokalia** but also the later representatives mentioned and quoted in the dialogues found here such as Saint Seraphim of Sarov and Bishop Ignatius Brianchaninov. If we do in fact have this opportunity, we do yet lack in the West, for the most part, that figure who fills these pages: the Staretz.* Rare among us are the Spiritual Fathers and Mothers, who from the fullness of their own life in the Spirit are able to foster the generation of spiritual life in others through their powerful mediatorial prayer, the daily practice of starchestvo,* and their words of life.

In the course of the Orthodox-Cistercian Symposium at Oxford University in 1973, the Cistercians lamented the lack of life-generating Spiritual Fathers and Mothers in the West today. In a moment of equal candor Bishop Antonie of Romania acknowledged that the Eastern Christians suffered in the same way. I asked Bishop Antonie what they did in the face of this lack, since the Spiritual Father or Mother occupies such a central role in Eastern Christian monasticism. The Bishop's response was an important one: We are to turn to the Fathers and Mothers who have gone before. They indeed are alive in the ever-present Lord. If we approach in faith, we can truly contact them and receive the instruction we need from them through their writings and the witness of them passed on to us by their disciples. Herein lies the pre-eminent value of this volume: it offers the opportunity of such life-giving contact.

As I share these pages, I feel a certain sadness at their very real inadequacy. People who study such things in the behavioral sciences tell us that when two persons converse, only a relatively small part of the communication is in their words. So much more is communicated by the personal presence, the feelings, emotions, and tone that hand, eye, and gesture, the whole body, bespeak. If that is generally true, how much more is it so in the case of these who so fully incarnate the Spirit of God. There is a veritable aura about them. Their eyes, so often washed by tears, are unsullied windows that let one look into a soul that is all afire, the welcoming warmth of a friendly hearth somehow beckoning even though one is in the presence of leaping flames of divine love. Words — the best — fall far short of capturing or conveying such spirit. But readers who have the same Spirit alive in them will bring their own source of fire to these recorded words, and as they read the words will again burst into fiery tongues to illumine and inflame. It is with this humble confidence that Brother Sergius and I share these words gathered over the years from many distant places, oftentimes from those who are no longer pilgrims but present to us as seers in Christ's love.

M. *Basil Pennington*

Spencer Abbey
Pentecost, 1978

COMMEMORATION

It is fitting that this volume so full of the wisdom of the Fathers and Mothers of Byzantine Christianity should be republished at this time. Not only does this respond to the interests and desires of many — a growing desire among us in the West to share something of the depths of a spirituality that belong to our common heritage — but it offers us an opportunity to pay tribute to a great pilgrim for Christian unity, Dr. Sergius Bolshakoff.

The Lord took his well-deserving servant to himself early this year (1991) as the universal church was celebrating the Octave of Church Unity. Sergius' peregrinations from monastery to monastery, sharing the wisdom of his heritage and weaving the bonds of unity, gradually slowed down in his declining years. He spent the last decade, the ninetieth of his life, at the Cistercian abbey of Hautrieve, near Fribourg in Switzerland. Right up to the hour of his death he continued his ministry through the pen, sharing his richly ladened memories in many languages and seeing that they were translated into still other languages. His bibliography is an impressive one, and all in service of deepening our lives in Christ and refinding our true unity in him.

It is good, then, as this servant of God and unity in God passes on, that this particularly rich collection of the wisdom he has garnered should once again be made widely available. Sensitive westerners will not always feel comfortable with some of the teaching emphasized by these Fathers and Mothers of Byzantine Christianity. But if we let them challenge us I am sure they will help us grow into a more integral and integrating Christian faith. In the depths they speak to the aspirations that are deepest in us all, as is witnessed by the popularity of this part of the Christian heritage in our times.

The situation of each of the communities described in these chapters has certainly evolved since the recounted interviews took place. Most of the Spiritual Fathers have gone to their reward. Mother Alexandra also completed her long and fruitful journey during the Church Unity Octave early this year. We would like to commemorate her in this new publication of her practical words of wisdom and offer a word of consolation to her daughters at Holy Transfiguration Monastery. The historical settings have changed but the serene guidance these holy men and woman have given us has a perduring value that interpenetrates all time.

Let us pray — as we all continue to develop and grow spiritually — that we can live in the spirit of these pages being fully open to the gift of wisdom which the words of this volume, imperfect thought they be, seek to impart.

Father M. Basil, OCSO

St. Joseph's Abbey
Pentecost, 1991

ACKNOWLEDGMENTS

First and above all we wish to express our gratitude, under God, to the revered Spiritual Fathers and Mother who so generously shared with us some of the divine wisdom they had received at such great price from the All-Merciful One. We are grateful to the Fathers and Mother who allowed us here to present their conferences, so full of light. We wish also to acknowledge the kindness of the Reverend Gareth M. Evans, Secretary of the Fellowship of Saint Alban and Saint Sergius, in giving us permission to use here the English translation of the conference of Archimandrite Vasileios and the account of Father Basil's visit to Archimandrite Aimilianos, which first appeared in their journal, *Sobornost*, and the editors of *Monastic Exchange* for the use of the translation of Archimandrite Sophrony's conference and the account of Father Basil's visit to him. A word of thanks, and more, are due also to Sister M. De Sales, OSB, for the patient and loving labor she put into the preparation of the manuscript. May the Savior of All bless and reward them.

CONTENTS

At the Lavra of
Saint Alexander Nevsky

Father Sergius

I met Father Sergius at the Lavra of Saint Alexander Nevsky when I was a schoolboy in St. Petersburg. Father Sergius was my confessor and I visited him occasionally. He had an apartment of several rooms, but he always received me in his study, with its two large windows and parquet floor. In one corner stood a bookstand with a cross and an epitrachelion,* which he donned to hear confessions. Many memories come to my mind when I think of the Lavra. I visited it often, beginning in 1908. Many of my relatives and friends of my family are buried in the cemetery of the Lavra, a true necropolis of the Empire. The Lavra was founded by Peter the Great in 1713, to be a model for other monasteries as well as a nursery of bishops. In the East, since the time of the early Ecumenical Councils, bishops are always monks.

Compared to other great Russian monasteries, the Lavra was unique in many respects. Usually, Russian monasteries had many unordained monks and relatively few priests, who served as confessors and celebrants at the Liturgy. In the Lavra there were in 1746 twenty-three priests and three deacons, with four lay monks and four novices. The priest-monks, or hieromonks,* were continually raised to the episcopate or sent as abbots to monasteries all over the Empire. Another characteristic of this Lavra in the eighteenth century was that many of its monks were originally professed in other monasteries and transferred to the Lavra in order to be prepared for high office. In this way, two monks of the Lavra, Innocent Kulchitsky and Sophrony

Nazarensky, were consecrated bishops of Iskartsk, in Siberia, and later canonized. Another monk of the Lavra, Father Theodore Ushakoff, became Superior of the famous Desert of Sanaskar, while Father Alexis Shestakov, a recluse, was the spiritual director of Czar Alexander I.

In due course, the office of Superior of the Lavra was united with that of the Metropolitan of St. Petersburg, the Primate of Russia. Among the prelates who held this post, Metropolitan Gabriel Petrov was perhaps the most remarkable. He introduced Orthodoxy into Alaska, which was then a Russian colony, and arranged to have the Greek *Philokalia* published in Old Slavonic. This greatly influenced the remarkable renewal of Russian monasticism in the nineteenth century. His successors, Metropolitans Michael Desbutzky, Seraphion Glagolev, and Isidore Nikolsky, were each remarkable in their own ways. The successor of Isidore Nikolsky, Metropolitan Pallady Raen, came from the province of Nizhny Novgorod. This was my mother's native province, and she knew the Metropolitan quite well.

At the time the Empire came to an end, the Lavra was an immense complex of magnificent baroque buildings with vast gardens. Besides the monastic community, it housed the Imperial Ecclesiastical Academy (the Faculty of Theology), the Seminary, the Palace of the Primate, and other institutions. The community was made up of cultured and wealthy men who live on the estate rather in the fashion found in the great monasteries of the French *ancien régime* on the eve of the revolution.

I often spoke with Father Sergius on prayer and the monastic life.

"You, Serezha, are interested in Valaam* and you are right," the hieromonk once said to me. "Their life is truly ascetical. They live on the islands and are completely cut off from the vanities of the world and its temptations. Silence and a harsh northern environment surround them. They are true cenobites,* and they also have hermits and recluses. Their Startzy teach them how to practice the Prayer of the Heart. Our life here is quite different. We live in the imperial capital, always with people, always with temptations. The Primate lives with us. The members of the Holy Synod often visit us. Archimandrites who are to be promoted to the episcopate spend their time of probation with us. Members of the imperial family, court dignitaries, government officials, diplomats, wealthy people, et cetera, come to us.

"Look around you and see how we live here. It is like being in a palace: self-contained apartments, parquet floors, servants. Our refectory is like a palatial banquet hall. Our food, although meatless, is very good. To the monks of Valaam all this is scandalous. They call us monks only by courtesy. And yet, Serezha, this isn't quite true. I agree of course that monks should live apart from the world, fasting and praying in solitude and not in the capital city and in comfort. Still the heart of the problem is not in these things but in the soul, in the interior castle. Of what use is it to live in the desert, as an early monastic Father said, if our hearts are full of memories of past humiliations or if we despise others? It is quite possible to live in our Lavra, among people, and still attain to true holiness.

"There was a man who lived in Constantinople in the days of the Byzantine Empire, who did just that and became a true saint. His name was Symeon. He was a wealthy aristocrat and lived in the capital all his life. Yet, thanks to prayer and a good life, he attained to great visions and transcendent wisdom and left remarkable writings. He is called the "New Theologian." The Church gives the title of "Theologian" to only three saints: Saint John the Evangelist, Saint Gregory of Nazianzus, and this Symeon. People can attain salvation everywhere and in any state of life. We also have our ascetics, but we do not publicize them. This is better."

"And who are they?" I asked.

"Father Theodore Ushakoff, for instance, Superior of the Desert of Sanaskar, in the diocese of Tambov. And the hieroschimonk* Alexis Shestakov, who lived during the reign of Alexander I. Have you heard of them, Serezha?"

Father went on to tell their story: John Ushakoff came from an ancient and noble family that gave several noted men to Russia. He was born in the province of Yaroslav, on the upper Volga. In due course he joined the Imperial Guard and served in St. Petersburg. Once, when he and his friends had dined too well, one of them suddenly dropped dead. This incident impressed the young man of twenty very forcefully. He realized the vanity and uncertainty of a worldly life and the fact that all must die. He understood the words "In whatever state I find you, I will judge you." Taking off his splendid uniform, John donned the garb of a beggar and left the capital without notifying anyone. He retired to the virgin forest of northern Dvina to take up the life of a hermit.

Because Ushakoff had left his regiment without permission, he was considered a deserter, albeit, an officer. Ushakoff could not remain for long in the Dvina forests, for they were full of deserters who were constantly pursued by the military police. He therefore moved southward, to Ploshansk Monastery. The abbot there could not receive him, because he was considered a deserter, but he gave him a hut in the neighboring forest for a hermitage. In 1745 Ushakoff was arrested as a deserter and sent to St. Petersburg to be punished. His case was reported to Empress Elizabeth, the pious daughter of Peter the Great. She pardoned Ushakoff and allowed him to become a professed monk in the Lavra in 1747. She herself was present at his profession.

Because Father Theodore, as John Ushakoff was called after his profession, was a spiritual director of rare quality, crowds started coming to him for advice and instruction. Some monks became jealous and began telling other monks of the Lavra that Father Theodore was seeking cheap popularity, unbecoming a monk. Faced with such fraternal jealousy, Father was allowed, in 1750, to retire to the celebrated monastery of Sarov, where Saint Seraphim was then living. In 1762 Father Theodore was ordained a priest and appointed Superior of Sanaskar Monastery. He did much for his monastery, but, unable to tolerate injustice, he severely criticized the local governor. Because of this criticism, the governor accused Father Theodore of fomenting a peasant rebellion. As a result, Father was confined for nine years in the ecclesiastical prison in the remote arctic Solovki Monastery, on an island in the White Sea.

When he was allowed to return to Sanaskar, Father Theodore again began to attract crowds of people, who came to him for instruction and counseling. At one period he also traveled to the Alexecusky Nunnery to confess and direct the sisters, but this was later forbidden him, again through envy. Father Theodore died in 1791. He might well be canonized, as was Saint Seraphim.

"Remember, Serezha," added the holy monk, "no one wishing to follow our Lord can escape sorrows and persecutions." Father Theodore could not escape such testing. He was persecuted through envy and because of his truthfulness. People dislike being reprimanded.

Father Sergius then spoke of another example, the hieromonk and recluse Alexis, known in the world as Alexander Shestakov. Father Alexis also lived at the Saint Alexander Nevsky Lavra, but sometime after Father Theodore. He was originally a serf and received his freedom only when he was sixty years old, in 1814. He first entered Savin-Storsjhevsky Monastery and then went to the Lavra of Saint Sergius of Radonezk, near Moscow. There he was speedily professed and ordained a priest on account of his remarkable spiritual qualities. Very soon, he became confessor and spiritual director to Seraphim Glagolev, Metropolitan of Moscow and Abbot of the Lavra. When Metropolitan Seraphim was appointed to the Russian primacy in St. Petersburg, he took his confessor with him. In 1823, Shestakov became megaloschemos,* with the name of Alexis.

In 1825, Emperor Alexander I came to the Lavra by night to consult Father Alexis before leaving for Taganrog, where he died. In spite of the fact that it was night, the Lavra community, headed by the Primate, met the Emperor at the gate with the bells ringing. A service of intercession was sung in the katholicon.* The Emperor venerated the relics of his ancestor, Saint Alexander Nevsky, Grand Duke of Vladimir. Afterward he went to see Father Alexis, accompanied by the Primate. The recluse had a peculiar cell. Its walls were covered with a black cloth halfway up. Before the wall stood a large crucifix with Our Lady and Saint John the Evangelist on either side. An oil lamp burned before the crucifix. Along another wall stood a long black bench. In the next room there was a black coffin covered with a black cloth. Nothing more.

"The saying is true, Serezha," continued the monk, " 'Remember your last end and you will never sin.' In youth this truth is forgotten, but old men know it well. When a man's conscience is pure he is joyful. If you have sinned you must repent on the spot. The difference between ordinary people and hardened criminals is simple. The first repent after they have sinned and try to amend their lives, while the second do not. Thus they become accustomed to sin and gradually lose the capacity to repent. Indeed a godly life appears to them unnatural and foolish. Did you ever visit the imperial graves in the fortress of Saint Peter and Saint Paul?" Father asked.

"Yes I did. My godfather, my maternal uncle, served in the Imperial Guard and was attached to the fortress for a while. I visited him occasionally with my father. I also visited the fortress with my *dyadka* (personal servant), Basil Suvorov, now a commissioned officer in the Grenadier Guard Regiment."

"Well, what did you see?"

"I was always astonished that so many people ordered the Panikhida (memorial service) before the tomb of the Emperor Paul and many pilgrims gathered around it. All the other tombs were visited only by tourists and the curious."

"You see, Serezha, God's ways are not ours. The voice of the people is the voice of the Lord." He went on: "How are the saints canonized? A saintly man dies. People begin to celebrate Panikhidi on his grave. They ask his intercession in various cases. For instance, people coming to the tomb of the Emperor Paul are either married couples in difficulties or those who have complicated court cases. Then people start to be healed through the intercession of the holy man. The coffin is opened and the relics exposed. When this happens the canonization is near. This happened with the canonization of Saint Tikhon of Zadonsk, Saint Innocent of Irkutsk and Saint Seraphim of Sarov. People in St. Petersburg venerate also the grave of the Blessed Xenior, Fool for Christ's sake, who died nearly one hundred and fifty years ago and was buried in the Smolensky churchyard. Did you go there?"

"No" I replied.

"Go," he said sharply. "You will find much to meditate upon."

"Was the Emperor Paul a saint?" I asked, rather astonished.

"God only knows that," he answered, "but if the people venerate his memory and ask his intercession, he most likely was. You saw this yourself. There is no veneration of any other emperor, even Alexander II, who abolished serfdom. The high circles tried many times to stop the public veneration of Paul I as a scandal, and failed. The life of that emperor was hard and sorrowful. He suffered much during his life and was finally murdered. No one can be saved living comfortably. Paul I died because he cared for the little and the oppressed and was hated by the strong and powerful.

"His son, Alexander I, all his life considered himself guilty of the death of his father, though perhaps he could not have prevented it. This guilty feeling troubled his conscience. Alexander I was handsome, charming, intelligent. He was successful in everything, yet he was always unhappy. He could not find peace of soul anywhere. After a long struggle he defeated Napoleon and entered Paris. He liberated many European countries conquered by Napoleon and made Russia the strongest continental power. And yet he never had peace of mind. Before leaving his capital for Taganrog, he came to the Lavra to consult Father Alexis. Alexander never returned to St. Petersburg. Officially he died in Taganrog. Some people, however, believe he did not die there but left for the Holy Land, while a soldier was buried in his stead in the fortress. It is also said that he returned to Russia afterward and died in Siberia as Staretz Theodore Kuznick. There is a certain amount of mystery here. These reports may be only rumors, but there is no smoke without fire.

"Keep your conscience pure, Serezha, and repent as soon as you have sinned. Pray often and read the Holy Scriptures and meditate upon them. That is all I have to say to you." And with this word of life, Father closed our last conversation.

I never met Father Sergius in later years. The Lavra was closed during the revolution and the community dispersed. The Metropolitan Benjamin Kazansky was executed in the twenties, as well as some monks. Others were deported to die in concentration camps. Father Sergius disappeared in those years. In 1960 I revisited the former imperial capital, renamed Leningrad. The Lavra of Saint Alexander Nevsky is now occupied by various Soviet institutions. There is no longer any monastic community there, though the Lavra still houses the Academy of Theology and the Seminary. And the Metropolitan still has his residence there. The katholicon, the Church of the Holy Trinity, has been restored to worship and is filled to overflowing on Sundays and feasts. This would, indeed, be a consolation to the humble Father who had given me so much good advice.

In the Tradition of
Bishop Ignatius

Hierodeacon Isaya Bobinin

Shortly after my arrival at the Pskovo-Petchersky Monastery in June 1926, my friend Novice Sergius Paulus brought to my cell a very lively little hierodeacon,* Father Isaya. Father was about forty at the time. His black hair made his brilliant, intelligent eyes even more striking. I have never forgotten that first meeting.

Father Isaya was of peasant origin, coming from Novgorod Province. Influenced by his grandmother and another old peasant, he early became attracted to religious life. The lives of holy monks, which were told and retold, impressed him, and he wanted to imitate them. Passing pilgrims told him of the monasteries they had visited, and this greatly increased his interest.

When Father Isaya reached eighteen, his parents gave him their blessing to enter the strict Novgorodian monastery in the Desert of Saint Macarios. Because there was no Staretz in the desert at that time, and therefore no possibility for starchestvo,* about which the young novice had learned from the writings of Bishop Ignatius Brianchaninov, he went to Valaam. There he was able to enter into the practice of hesychasm.

The Staretz, or Elder, is a director of conscience and a novice master combined. He is selected by the Hegumen* from among the monks renowned for their wisdom, learning, and mystical experience.

The postulants, novices, and professed monks are under his direction. They surrender their wills to him and do nothing without his permission. The Staretz traces for them the whole program of life they must follow, and every evening they come to him to confess their thoughts and deeds and to receive his instructions. The highest spiritual perfection is often reached by monks living under an experienced and saintly Staretz. The Prayer of Jesus is commonly used to reach the height of Christian perfection. This exercise consists in repeating devoutly, in appropriate conditions, this short prayer: Jesus Christ, Son of God, have mercy on me, a sinner. This prayer, repeated with certain approved meditations, leads eventually to the recognition of one's own nothingness and to the complete and joyful trust in Divine Providence. It is combined frequently with many other ascetical exercises. Instead of the Prayer of Jesus, which is inspired by the prayer addressed to our Lord by the blind Bartimaeus (Mark 10:46 f.), any other short prayer may be used. The essence of the method consists in the realization of that constant Divine Presence which speedily leads to the practice of virtue and the contemplation of the highest truths. The Prayer of Jesus was introduced, or better reintroduced, into Russia by the disciples of Father Paisios Velichkovsky, a Russian himself, who lived in eighteenth-century Romania. This practice is very old.

After a few years in Valaam, Father Isaya was transferred to the household of Archbishop Anthony of Tver, who, being a monk himself, held in greatest respect those of Valaam, and periodically obtained trained novices for his monasteries from the Superior of Valaam. This time, the Hegumen selected Father Isaya and sent him to Tver, where he remained for a short time. Then, trained and experienced, he returned to Saint Macarios Monastery to be professed there. Valaam and Tver were for him only a training ground. His novitiate lasted several years and included training in three monasteries.

Usually in the Orthodox Church the novitiate or probation lasts three years, but it may be prolonged. In Russia, an aspirant to the religious life visits a Hegumen and requests permission to try his vocation. The Hegumen, after deliberation, accepts the newcomer and hands him over to one of the Elders, or experienced monks, to be initiated into the religious life. The probationer receives a robe and starts to grow a beard. He is called *poslushnik* (one learning to obey). Sometime after three years of probation, the Hegumen tonsures the novice, changes his name, and gives him certain articles of the monastic habit, including the *mandorrhason*, or *pallium*, a wide-sleeved cloak. He then becomes a rhasophore,* bearer of the rhason.* Henceforth he is incorporated in the monastic body and may not leave the monastery, although he has not as yet made any vows.

The next stage is the profession for life, usually at the age of thirty for a man and forty for a woman. The rhasophore pronounces four vows: stability, obedience, poverty, and chastity, by giving the affirmation replies to the express questions of the Hegumen, but without signing any formula as Westerners do. Then the rhasophore is tonsured and receives the little habit, including the mandyas (an ample cloak) and the taramandyas (similar to the Latin little scapular). The monk is now called stavrophore,* because he wears a wooden cross. The ceremony of profession is very beautiful.

Most of the monks, indeed an overwhelming majority, do not proceed to the last degree of angelical perfection, that of the skhimnik* or megaloschemos. No one is made skhimnik in Russia before passing thirty years as a stavrophore and being renowned for his piety. The skhimnik is usually professed by a bishop in a most beautiful and touching ceremony. He receives a special dress, which includes the koukkoulion, a veiled head covering, and the analabos, or scapular. Fully dressed, the skhimnik looks quite similar to the Benedictine monk, except that his scapular is embroidered with the instruments of the Passion of Christ. Severe fasts and long prayers are prescribed for the skhimnik, who usually becomes a solitary or a recluse and sometimes a Staretz.

Father Isya lived peacefully in his monastery, and even the fall of the Russian Empire did not disturb him much.

Bolshevism changed things very little during the first years. To conform to the new law forbidding the ownership of land by ecclesiastical persons, the monastery was registered as an agricultural commune owned by the novices and employing the monks as hired laborers. Meanwhile the torrent of the revolution rushed onward with full speed in the great world outside the monastery. On October 28, 1917, the great Patriarchate of Moscow, suppressed by Peter the Great in 1720, was restored, and Metropolitan Tikhon of Moscow was elected in the old Kremlin as the Patriarch of all Russia to rule over one hundred and ten million Orthodox. He was an anti-Bolshevik and condemned the Communists and their teaching in his very first encyclical. The Bolsheviks, too weak as yet to molest the Church, left it in comparative peace until the civil war was over. Then, in 1922, they started their first anti-religious drive, under the pretext that the clergy were unwilling to submit to the spoliation of churches. The great famine that broke out in Russia as a result of communism furnished the Bolsheviks with the pretext to confiscate the Church's treasures, including sacred vessels, in order to sell them abroad in exchange for food for the starving provinces. The Patriarch agreed to deliver these vessels, but in an orderly way and with a guarantee that the proceeds would be used properly. The Bolsheviks rejected his offer and imprisoned the bishops and laymen who resisted them. Many of the clergy were executed shortly afterward, including the saintly Benjamin Kazanski, Metropolitan of Petrograd. The Roman Catholic clergy resisted likewise: Archbishop Cipelac was arrested and Monsignor Budkevich executed. Patriarch Tikhon himself was subsequently imprisoned. His imprisonment led the Russian Church into difficulties that ended in the wholesale persecution of Christians of all denominations. When the Patriarch and most of the diocesan bishops were suddenly arrested, some priests, ingratiating themselves with the Soviets and strongly imbued with Bolshevism, supported by Bishop Antonin Granovski, seized the opportunity to proclaim the Patriarch deposed and to form a temporary administration of the Russian Church presided over by Bishop Antonin. Later this group of Renovators became known as the Living Church.

The schismatic society was really quite moderate in its views, judging by the then existing standards. They proclaimed their conviction that the Soviet regime had come to stay for several decades if not for centuries, and therefore the Church should try to conform to it. They also expressed their belief in the urgent need to modernize the canons and rites of the Russian Church to make it more comprehensible to the younger generation. They did not wish to change the dogmas. The Patriarch and his successors were constrained in due course to realize many aims of the Living Church, except its extreme innovations, such as the married episcopacy, marriage after ordination, and new Services.

The chief unpardonable sin of the Living Church was rebellion against the Patriarch, which broke the unity of the Russian Church for several years and thereby enabled the Bolsheviks to develop their enormous godless propaganda to reduce gradually to utter impotence not only all groups within the Russian Church but also the Roman Catholics and Protestants, who were too weak to defend themselves.

At the beginning of the Soviet revolution, Father Isaya, who was always of an ardent nature, entered into the struggle with the Renovators. As a result of his activities, he was arrested, imprisoned, and sentenced to deportation to Siberia. He managed, however, to escape, crossed the Estonian border, and was received into the monastic community of Pskovo-Petchersky. After a time, he was ordained to the diaconate.

Father Isaya was a great admirer of Bishop Ignatius Brianchaninov, whom he preferred to that other great Russian contemplative Bishop Theophan the Recluse. He knew the *Philokalia*, the Sayings of the Fathers, and the lives of many saints, especially Russian, practically by heart. The Holy Scriptures and the Fathers were always on his lips. Father Isaya was my first guide in the practice of the Jesus Prayer.

One wonderful June morning in 1926 I was sitting with him on a bench in the monastery garden. The blue dome of heaven was cloudless. Many birds were singing in the trees. The air was pure and perfumed with the fragrance of the blossoming flowers. The ancient churches of the monastery, with their small bulbous domes and shining gilded crosses were visible through the thick greenery of the flowering *cheremukha*.

"Tell me, Father Isaya, how Bishop Ignatius understood the Prayer of Jesus. He was a very cultured man."

"Yes he was indeed. According to Bishop Ignatius, the practice of the Prayer of Jesus is the bounden duty of all Orthodox, which they must not neglect. However, the external prayer alone is not enough as Saint Seraphim of Sarov always insisted. God listens to our mind. Therefore, those who do not unite the external prayer with the inner one are not truly praying."

"Tell me, Father, how one starts to practice the Prayer of Jesus."

"In order to begin the practice of the Prayer of Jesus, the Bishop teaches us, we must first lead a wise and abstemious life, avoiding all luxuries and all carnal pleasure. We must watch over our sight, hearing, and other senses and limit our speech to the needful. This does not mean, however, that we should all retire into a solitude. He who truly learns the Prayer of Jesus learns well how to live in a true solitude. Several Fathers, like Alexis the Man of God, Saint John the Tent-liver, and Saint Vitalius, practiced the ascesis of solitude of the heart and a true seclusion while still living in the world."

"Then what do we do?"

"We must first master our passions. This is done by frequent vocal prayer and psalmody. Then we may dare to practice mental prayer. Otherwise we may easily fall into spiritual illusion and diabolic temptations, have visions, hear voices, and so on. When we practice the Prayer of Jesus and any other kind of prayer, we should seek to acquire that special form of humility called *plach*, or lamentation. This is the sentiment of deep repentance of heart — salutary sorrow for committed sins and for our multifarious human weaknesses. This lamentation, or tears, is the only sacrifice that God accepts from fallen humanity before our soul is fully restored by the Holy Ghost through transfiguration. The penitential lamentation destroys passions, as fire burns dead wood, and introduces into our soul joy and serenity.

"Bishop Ignatius teaches us that prayer without penance, neglectful and self-interested, always leads to spiritual illusions, especially in the case of those who are inclined to daydreaming and have powerful imaginations. Progress in prayer is difficult. When you practice the Prayer of Jesus yourself, you will find that this is so. The prayer of attention demands self-sacrifice. They are few in number who are ready for this. We must have a true sorrow for our sins.

"And take note of this, my friend. The general sign of all spiritual states is deep humility, humble wisdom, setting our neighbor's good before our own, evangelical love of our neighbor, desire to be unknown and to leave behind worldly vanity. He who attains to true prayer experiences indescribable poverty of spirit when he stands up before the Lord God in prayer and presents to him his requests."

"This is true, Father Isaya. I have always realized that those who practice true prayer do want to go apart, to be unknown, to leave behind all worldly vanity."

"We must pray, dear Brother Sergius, with great attention, because when our mind is attentive then our heart responds with tenderness. Then only is prayer the common expression of both mind and heart together. The words of prayer should be said slowly in order that our mind can understand them, enter into the words of prayer. You can read all this in the writings of Bishop Ignatius."

"This is true for prayer in general, Father Isaya. What can you say of the Prayer of Jesus?"

"The same. The Prayer of Jesus is usually this: 'Lord Jesus Christ, Son of God, have mercy on me, a sinner.' We must say it first vocally. Then the vocal prayer will transform itself into mental prayer in due time. We should pronounce the Prayer in a low tone to be heard by none but ourselves. When we are overpowered by distractions, boredom, sadness, or the like, then we should pronounce our Prayer loudly — when we are alone in our cell. Vocal prayer awakens our soul from its heavy sleep caused by sorrow and boredom.

"When we experience an invasion of all kinds of thoughts and carnal desires, the best thing to do is to pray loudly. Slow and deep breathing while we pray helps to keep our attention concentrated."

"When should I do this?"

"Now; when you start to pray in your cell. Make your own private rule how many bows and prostrations you should make. Those bows when your head is brought to the level of your belt as well as the great metanias,* or prostrations, should be done slowly, with sentiments of repentance. Say the Prayer of Jesus with each bow, standing in one place, keeping yourself recollected. Start with twelve bows. Do not increase their number vainly. We must do everything gradually."

"I heard, Father Isaya, of the Prayer of the Heart. What is it?"

"Do not try to find it, but practice solely penitential prayer. In due course you will find the place of the heart. When you feel within you poverty of spirit, tenderness of heart, and tears, you may take it for granted that you are making progress in the right way. It is certainly good to have as a guide a Staretz who has experience in the practice of the Prayer of Jesus and who is able to give you good advice."

Such was my first interview with Father Isaya.

Our second meeting took place a few days later in the upper garden of the monastery, from which one could see a vast panorama of fields and woods extending eastward into the Soviet Union.

"What do you think, Father, of the present state of the Russian Church? Can she survive the present trial?"

"She will certainly survive, my friend. The Russian Church has several wise and young bishops, like Bishop Alexis Simansky, auxiliary of Novgorod, whom I often met when I was caring for the affairs of the Desert of Saint Macarios, or Bishop Nicholas Garushevich of Peterhof, with whom I shared the struggle with the Renovators."

"And the Renovators, Father Isaya; will they remain or disappear?"

"They will disappear. Now in Russia there is a crisis of faith and the triumph of atheists. We can fight the crisis only with prayer and sacrificial living. The Renovators believed that they would establish themselves by flattering the government and with crafty speeches and vain talk before the believers. The latter see that the Renovators are opportunists who look for power and a comfortable living. They are indulgent toward human desires and passions, because they are mastered by them. They consecrate married priests as bishops and allow second marriages to the secular clergy. They abolished monastic vows, pretending that they are against nature. The Renovators lack humility, prayer, and simplicity. They look for an easier life on this earth. It is not the way of Christ, the way of the Cross."

"Can we continue our last talk, Father Isaya?"

"Why not? Bishop Ignatius distinguishes two stages in the practice of the Prayer of Jesus, which lead us to impassibility. During the first stage we pray with effort, continually rejecting distracting thoughts and the attacks of passion. This is the time of labor. The second stage starts when we feel the presence of Divine Grace. The mind is now united with the heart. This is the 'Prayer of the Heart.' Prayer becomes free of distractions and is accompanied with tender, penitential tears. Sinful thoughts lose their mastery over the mind, and life runs on serenely.

"At this time we should develop in ourselves humility and obedience to our Spiritual Father. The latter frees us from all cares. He who acquires true *humility* cannot be mastered by transitory things. He is freed from all sorrow and the burden of cares, which can distract our minds and make our prayer fruitless. Only a very few attain solitude of mind, but we should not be depressed. Let us pray continually and patiently, and the Lord will grant us in due course the pure Prayer of Grace. He who prays persistently with his impure prayer, never falling into depression when he sees no results, will attain in time pure, undistracted prayer.

"Bishop Ignatius states that the first fruits of prayer are attention and sweetness. The latter is born of the first. The sweet feeling of tenderness steadies the attention. Influencing each other, attention and tenderness make prayer deep and pure, suppress distractions and daydreaming, and make our hearts lively. Attention and sweetness, like true prayer, are gifts of God. By forcing ourselves to pray, we show our desire to acquire prayer, while our efforts to attain to attention and to tenderness demonstrate our will to gain them.

"The next fruit of prayer is an every-increasing capacity to see our sins and our sinfulness. This increases our delicacy of feeling and leads to tears. Lamentations are an overflowing tenderness of heart united with the sorrow of a humble and penitential heart. These tears proceed from the depths of the heart and envelop the soul. When the man of prayer receives this gift of tears, he is overshadowed by the Divine Presence, death is very present to him, and he fears judgment and condemnation. As he continues to progress, the man of prayer is penetrated with a refined, holy, and spiritual sense of the fear of God. This sensation cannot be likened to any other sensation of the carnal or even of the merely spiritual man. This is something new. This fear of God melts passions, while mind and heart are irresistibly attracted to uninterrupted prayer.

"In time the contemplative attains a state of tranquility, humility, and a love of God and neighbor, without distinguishing the good and the bad. At the same time, the soul acquires the ability to endure the sorrows permitted by God to heal his vices and to help him overcome his sinfulness. The love of God and neighbor, born from the fear of God, is radically different from merely human love. It is altogether spiritual, holy, refined, and humble.

"Bishop Ignatius advises us to keep in our cells large icons of the Savior and of the Mother of God. They help us to realize better the presence of God and to behave accordingly. He also said that, once we begin our rule of prayer, it is inadmissible to abandon it, especially for long periods. It is better not to begin the exercises of prayer than to begin and then give them up. Into the soul that abandons the blessed alliance with prayer, passions flow as an irresistible flow and over-power it. The invading passions receive special power over such a soul. They install themselves solidly in such a soul and can hardly be overcome afterward. Unbelief, cruelty, hardness of heart penetrate the soul. Devils once expelled by prayer return, burning with vengeance for their exile and in a greater number. According to the Gospel, the last state of such a person is worse than the first.

"It is for this reason that the fate of apostates is so terrible. They become toys of the devil, full of evil, blasphemy, cruelty, despair, boredom. I witnessed many such cases during my struggle with the Renovators and with militant godless men in the courts and in prison."

"Tell me, Father Isaya, since you know so well the teachings of Bishop Ignatius, how have you applied them in your own life?"

"I have tried, of course, especially when I lived in Valaam and in my Novgorodian monastery. Later on, when the revolution came and propagandists started to visit our monastery and to corrupt novices and even monks, I was forced to fight with them and to plunge into a sea of evil and hatred. They are infectious. While we are little able to do good, to practice humility, patience, and meekness, it is easy to pay eye for eye, tooth for tooth. I believe it is better for a monk to remain in his cell and to converse with God than to move about in the world. The ancient Fathers rightly said that a monk who often leaves his cell for business' sake returns in a worse state, full of worldly impressions and passions. By necessity I used often to leave my Novgorodian monastery, and I learned by experience the truth of the Fathers' warnings."

In the days that followed, I often met with Father Isaya to speak of various problems connected with the practice of the Prayer of Jesus. He taught me all he knew. I stayed three months in Pskovo-Petchersky Monastery. I always recall those months with gratitude. I arrived in the beginning of June, at the end of spring, when *cheremukha* and lilacs were blooming. The days were warm and sunny, perfumed and still. I used to talk also with the Hegumen, Bishop John Bulin, Auxiliary of the Metropolitan of Estonia, as well as with other monks, and with the novices, especially Brother Sergius Paulus.

I left the ancient monastery one marvelous autumn evening in the beginning of September 1926. Father Isaya and Brother Sergius accompanied me to the station. After taking leave of the Hegumen, we climbed into a horse-drawn carriage. Father Isaya took the driver's place, while Brother Sergius sat with me. Father Isaya took the reins and the horses started to trot. We crossed ourselves, according to custom. We went up the hill to the Holy Gates of the monastery. I looked back. Ancient churches, white, cream, and pink, stood out boldly on the bright green background. The gilded crosses on the domes shone in the sunset. We passed through the gates, and the ancient Pskovo-Petchersky monastery dropped out of my sight for thirty-four years. I saw it again only in July 1960.

The train was already in the station. I said good-by to Father Isaya and to Brother Sergius. I never saw them again. Brother Sergius died in the forties, while Father Isaya went to the Holy Land shortly after my departure. He settled in Jericho. I corresponded with him occasionally till the Second World War broke out. During the hostilities, he also died. But his holy words remain firmly in my memory, very much alive, and bring me untold good.

Father Theophan and the Pskovo-Petchersky Monastery

The university town of Tartu, in Estonia, where I lived for a few years after I left Russia in 1922, was founded in 1030 by Yaroslav the Wise, Grand Duke of Russia. In 1224 it was seized by German knights and renamed Dorpat. Some Russian merchants and artisans, however, remained in the town and formed two parishes. The relations between the Russians and the Germans were variable but on the whole satisfactory. Although two Crusades were preached to subdue the Russian Orthodox and make them Latins, they were both unsuccessful and did not embitter the mutual relations unduly. The Swedes were routed near modern Leningrad on July 15, 1240, by Saint Alexander Nevsky, Grand Duke of Russia, who also destroyed the German crusaders on the ice covering Lake Peipus, in Estonia, on April 5, 1242. Six years later, Pope Innocent IV sent two legates to Saint Alexander, urging him to join the Roman Church, but the embassy came to naught. The memories of the Fourth Crusade and the sacking of Constantinople by the Latins in 1204 were yet too fresh in the minds of the Orthodox.

After the final failure of the Swedes to subdue the Russians a century later, relations were stabilized and became even friendly. The Latins were allowed to have churches and monasteries in several commercial cities of the Russian North, such as Novgorod, Pskov, and Ladoga. Some Latin monks even helped Archbishop Gennadius of Novgorod (1485-1505) to combat the Judaizers, a heretical sect, practicing Jewish rites, that appeared in Russia in the fifteenth century.

The Archbishop needed a complete Slavonic translation of the Old Testament to confound the heretics. As he was unable to obtain complete Greek or Slavonic Bibles, he was obliged to make his translation from the Vulgate. It was the Dominican Friar Benjamin, a Slovene by extraction, who, with the help of his nephew, did this for the Archbishop, translating some books of the Old Testament from the Vulgate in 1493. The Bible of Archbishop Gennadius was the only Slavonic Bible in Russia until Prince Constantine Ostrogski published another, in 1580. In his edition the Prince retained much from the Bible of Gennadius. As a result, up to the present time the Russian Church still uses at its Services a Bible some books of which were translated from the Vulgate by the Dominican Friar Benjamin. The Friar also wrote for the Archbishop a long sermon against those who oppress the Church.

Sometimes, however, the relations were disturbed by local incidents. The story of Tartu is one of them. Although by the Treaty of 1443 the Latin Bishop of Dorpat had agreed to allow the Russians to keep two parishes of their rite in the city, he in fact so oppressed them that one parish soon closed, and its priest, Father John, retired to the Russian principality of Pskov. There he took up his abode near the grotto where a solitary, Saint Marc, had lived. When the wife of Father John became a nun, he, too, entered the religious life and founded a monastery later known as the Pskovo-Petchersky Monastery. Its monastic church was consecrated on August 15, 1477. Meanwhile the pastor of the remaining Russian parish in Tartu, Father Isidore, was arrested with seventy-two companions by order of the Latin Prince-Bishop. They were all drowned on January 8, 1472, because of their refusal to accept the Latin rite. Isidore was canonized as a martyr, and a chapel was dedicated to him in the collegiate church of Tartu. By a strange coincidence, there is also a chapel there dedicated to Saint Josaphat Kunzevich, a well-known martyr for union with Rome, who died in White Russia during the seventeenth century. The Tartu incident was finally settled peacefully, and a new treaty restored to the Russians their former privileges.

Pskovo-Petchersky Monastery developed very slowly but in time became fully established.

The deep, solemn tone of the abbey bell roused me from sleep refreshed and joyful. The air was pure and invigorating. Drops of dew sparkled like diamonds on the grass, the leaves, and the flowers. In the sunshine of the early morning, against the background of a pale blue sky and verdant trees, the cream-white buildings with their many domes and campaniles rose before me like a fantasy — the city of Kitiesh come to life, as it were. Everything was ethereal, full of unearthly beauty. Holy Russia lived again. I was taken to the days of its glory. All things unpleasant — even the war, revolutions, and exile — disappeared like smoke on an autumn day. For me the Pskovo-Petchersky Monastery was a true Kitiesh — the legendary town in northern Russia that disappeared in a lake when the Mongolians besieged it in the thirteenth century. The Holy Lake is still there amid the Volga forests, and according to the legend, a man with a pure heart may find the entrance to the city. I found the entrance to my own "Kitiesh."

In the old katholicon, carved in the rock of the hill, the monks arranged themselves in a semicircle before the venerated icon of our Lady. The Hegumen-Bishop stood in the center. "Blessed be the Kingdom of the Father and of the Son and of the Holy Ghost," intoned the celebrant with a strong, solemn voice. Prayers and hymns alternated. The monks sang well, using old melodies similar to those of Western plain chant. Each word of the psalms was uttered clearly and slowly, and the mind willingly followed in joyful meditation.

After the Service, Father Vassian, the confessor of the community, began the celebration of the Liturgy.* On that "Kitiesh" morning, I realized for the first time the deep mystical beauty of the Liturgy, although I had participated in it hundreds of times before. As I contemplated the solemn rites, I sensed beneath them the mysteries of Calvary and the Resurrection. The fine old church, the carved and gilded iconostasis,* the delicately embroidered seventeenth century vestments, the heavenly singing, made the whole celebration extraordinarily beautiful. I beheld the venerable priest, whose gray eyes mirrored visions of glory accessible only to contemplatives who are called by special Divine Grace.

In the afternoon, Brother Sergius showed me the numberless wonders of the monastery: its churches and chapels, its sacristy and library, its cells and catacombs, its towers and gardens. I was impressed most of all by the monastic catacombs or grottoes — long galleries in the rock behind the old katholicon. Carved in the sandstone, they are broad, high, and airy. Many thousands of monks and a few laymen are buried there. The coffins are usually placed in an opening in the wall, which is then sealed with a tablet on which is engraved the name of the deceased and the date of his death. In a small chapel near the entrance there are three sarcophagi, enshrining the relics of Saints Marc, Jonas, and Vassa. Another chapel, deep in the rock, contains the coffins of several Hegumens and Recluses, including that of Father Theodosios, the last occupant of my cell. The coffins rested directly on the floor and were covered with a pall. A solemn, comforting silence reigned in this chapel deep within the rock. The air was fresh and pure, with a faint aroma of violets. The candles burned quietly. Under the purple velvet palls, in plain oak coffins, slept the Servants of God. The horror of death was absent; there was no nauseating odor, no terrifying mask on the face of the dead. Whenever these coffins have been opened, the bodies of the Servants of God have been found intact, their faces serene and venerable. It is difficult to described the atmosphere of this chapel. One feels transported to another world, entirely different from this world of ours, one that is radiant and peaceful.

I first met Father Theophan in Pskovo-Petchersky Monastery in 1926. He was then about seventy years old. A peasant from the province of Pskov, he had become a widower early in life but did not remarry. After seeing his only daughter married to a peasant from the same district and leaving all his property to her, the widower retired to Pskovo-Petchersky Monastery, where in due course he was professed under the name of Theophan. He was a very good monk. He loved prayer and work. For humility's sake he declined being prepared for ordination.

When my friend Father Isaya Babinin entered the Pskovo-Petchersky Monastery, he and Father Theophan became close friends and often met to discuss problems of spirituality. They had much in common: a peasant background, a love for reading, and piety. Father Isaya introduced me to Father Theophan and we used to meet often, usually in the garden of the monastery. Father Theophan loved to read, especially the writings of Bishop Theophan the Recluse. I believe it was in honor of the Recluse that he received the monastic name of Theophan.

Once when I was conversing with the old monk in the garden he said: "Well, Sergei Nikolaevich, the most important activity in life is unceasing prayer. We must pray always: when we rise, when we walk, when we eat — always, on every occasion. And we must pray with attention and feeling. To every appeal to pray we should say within ourselves: 'My heart is ready.' And we should not stop praying until our hunger is satisfied. Our whole life should be a continuous prayer. For every activity there is a proper time, but for prayer the time is *always*, just as for breathing. Our prayer and breathing should be united: every breath a prayer. I speak of the Prayer of the Heart, of which Father Isaya told you."

"That is the Prayer of Jesus?"

"It is. But we may very well compose our own short prayers, as did Saint Tikhon of Zadonsk. For example: 'Lord, teach me! Lord, give me understanding! Lord, help me!' And we should do this in fear and trembling. Especially should we thank and glorify God for the greatness and richness of his mercy. We should beg for understanding of how to live according to the Divine Will; if we do, it will be revealed to us. To ask for wealth, power, honors, or things of that kind would be to create idols. It is better not to ask for a wife, or children, or health, or a long life, because we do not know if such things are good for us. Nor should we persist in asking if the Lord does not give us what we have asked for a long time. If we persist, the Lord might grant our request to our own sorrow. If the Lord does not grant our request for a long time it may mean that what we ask for would be harmful to ourselves or to others. The only thing we should ask for persistently is stated in the Our Father: 'Thy will be done.'"

At that moment a monk appeared in the distance, slowly coming our way. "Who is he?" I asked.

"That is Father Vassian, our community's confessor," he answered; "a true Staretz, though he is younger than I. True wisdom is acquired not by long life but by life in Christ. So it is with Father Vassian. He came to us when still quite young. Though he is now a hieromonk and our community confessor, Father Vassian, like the Apostle Paul, works with his own hands. Some monks believe that if one becomes a hieromonk one is excused from hard manual labor and his business is to command other people. But this is not so."

Father Theophan went on to relate this story: Filaret Amfiteatrov, Metropolitan of Kiev, was a member of the Holy Synod and the recipient of the Grand Cross of Saint Andrew and other distinctions. He was even received into the Imperial Family. But he experienced many sorrows in his life. He was persecuted by those who disliked his ascetical ways and his stand for truth. Yet he never complained. His innocence was recognized and he was rapidly promoted.

One time when he traveled from Kiev to St. Petersburg to attend a session of the Holy Synod, the Metropolitan was crossing the province of Kursck. As was customary in those days, when railways were rare, he traveled in a coach with an escort. On the way, the Metropolitan wanted to visit a monastery about which he had heard a great deal. Because his heavy coach moved very slowly, Metropolitan Filaret went ahead alone in a peasant cart, dressed as usual as a simple monk, without any sign of his dignity. He arrived at the monastery just as the early Liturgy was beginning in the church. It was sung, on the occasion, in a side chapel. There were only a few people present, among them an important-looking hieromonk. When the time came for the Little Entrance with the Gospel text, there was no one to carry the candle before the priest. The Metropolitan turned to the hieromonk and said: "Father, take the candle and walk before the priest." The dignified hieromonk answered coolly: "I am a hieromonk and not an acolyte. Go and carry the candle yourself." The Metropolitan obeyed and walked before the celebrant with the candle.

At the end of the Service there was a commotion in the church. The Archimandrite came in, dressed as for a great occasion, followed by the senior members of his Synod. They all went directly to the Metropolitan and welcomed him according to custom. The pompous hieromonk realized then that the "monk" he had haughtily told to function as acolyte was the Metropolitan of Kiev! He was much abashed, but the Metropolitan in his kindness said nothing.

While Father Theophan was narrating this incident, Father Vassian arrived. "The Lord bless you, friends," he said, taking his seat on the bench. "What are you speaking about?"

Father Theophan answered: "I am telling Sergei Nikolaevich here that we must strive to pray always, and with humility."

"You do well to discuss spiritual things and not judge others. Alas, because of our sins, even in monasteries we often fail and begin to make judgments that are reserved to the Lord alone." The Staretz then took up Father Theophan's theme: "It is true, we must pray with prudence and confidence, asking for nothing worldly. The Lord knows better than we do what is useful for us. We must surrender ourselves to Divine Providence always and everywhere. This is true wisdom. The longer I live the more I see how the Lord guides us at all times, leading us toward good and holy things and destroying in us everything earthly and all our evil inclinations. In order to pray with attention, we must preserve a fear of God. He who always keeps in mind his death and the judgment of Christ will not sin easily. All this is very simple."

"Your monastery is idiorrhythmic* Father Vassian?" I observed. "Valaam is truly cenobitic,* is it not?"

"That is true, Sergei Nikolaevich. Because of our sins we are surrounded by a world of vanities. When monks have money of their own it is difficult to avoid envy and the love of material things. Yet even here it is possible to attain salvation. We also have had blessed Startzy. There was Father Lazar, with whom Alexander the First corresponded, and later Staretz Theodosios, whose cell you now occupy."

Father then gave this teaching: "One can be saved anywhere and one can also perish anywhere. Satan was the highest angel, standing always before God, and yet he fell by pride. Judas the Iscariot was one of the twelve Apostles, and yet because of his love for money he betrayed the Lord and afterward committed suicide. A good many people have perished in like manner. On the other hand, the sinful publican was justified by one short prayer. The good thief, already crucified, was saved too by one short prayer and entered paradise together with the Lord Himself. Our Lord told the proud, avaricious scribes and Pharisees that the publicans and the whores would go into the kingdom of God before them, because they repented at the preaching of Saint John the Baptist, whereas the proud teachers did not."

"But penance must be not only in words but in deeds as well, Father Vassian?"

"Of course. We are saved by deeds and not merely by words. The Savior himself once said: 'These people come to me saying: "Lord, Lord," but their heart is far from me.' Certainly, according to Saint Paul, it is impossible to please God without faith, but we must not forget Saint James, who asserted that faith without works is dead, and that even the devils believe and tremble, but they do nothing of merit."

"Father Vassian," I said, "many people nowadays assert that devils do not exist and that we sin only because of our own defects and passions."

"Yes, people who are supposed to be learned often say things like that, but they are truly unwise." The Father shared some of his wisdom: "Devils always try to persuade their victims that they do not exist, because if they do not exist it is useless to struggle with them. We can then rest easy with our defects and passions and even be condescending toward them, arguing that they are ingrained in us, inseparable from our perverted nature. Whether devils exist or not, we can learn by personal experience. Only try to lead a truly Christian life, and temptations and troubles of all kinds will assail you. It is true, as wise men say, that there is a devil assigned to every Christian to tempt him; but to a monk, two are assigned. Devils seduce us to sin by filling our imaginations with daydreams and fantasies. Satan dreamed of being equal to God, and fell. Likewise Judas. We must avoid, at all cost, daydreaming and laziness. While working, we must occupy our mind with the Prayer of Jesus. If we do this, devils find no place near us and we need not fear them. They are not all-powerful.

"It is also true that a heart completely free of daydreams and fantasies gives birth to thoughts both divine and mysterious which play about in it as dolphins in a still, sun-bathed sea.

"Well, friends, I must go on my way," Father Vassian said as he rose and quietly started down the path.

"How right he is, dear Sergei Nikolaevich," Father Theophan observed, and he added his own thoughts: "We must be afraid of all daydreams, fantasies, and illusions and fill our heart with the invocation of the Divine Name. And yet we all dream, always waiting for something, even in our old age. The young dream all the time. They dream of having a prosperous life, full of pleasures, honors, riches, and power. And in order to attain such a life they resort to lies and flattery and become hard and cruel. There are, of course, many exceptions, but such is the rule. Do you know, Sergei Nikolaevich, that old age is better than youth? And why? Because it is wiser. In old age we realize at last that all is vanity. 'Vanity of vanities and all things are vanity,' as the Ecclesiast says. Everything passes away: our youth, our health, our relatives and our friends, our foes, our wealth, and our honors. Only peace of mind, good deeds, and eternity remain."

Father Theophan died a few years after I left Pskovo-Petchersky Monastery. His end was peaceful, without suffering, without a struggle. Father Vassian became a megaloschemos, receiving the name Symeon. He died at the ripe old age of ninety-three a couple of years before my visit to Pskovo-Petchersky Monastery in 1960. He sang Liturgy daily and worked in his shop till the very end. They told me he died without any suffering; he just fell asleep to wake in another world.

It may not always be easy to live as a monk, but to die as a monk, a good monk who has seen the great Light and walked in his radiance — that is true blessedness.

Hieromonk Dorofey
of Konevitsa

The First Steps
on the Spiritual Journey

I first met Father Dorofey in the Monastery of Konevitsa, in Finland, in the summer of 1954. It touches a certain chord in my heart when I think of that small monastery lost in the vast forests of the North: the forests and the lakes, the lakes in the forests. Stillness, giant conifers, the tranquil lakes. Konevitsa always reminded me of the Skete of Saint Nilos Maikov, on the river Sorska in the dense forests of the Rostov country.

The few small houses that made up the Skete stood out on the slope of the hill by the lake. On the edge of the meadow there was a primitive clock tower, I myself lived in a log cabin at the edge of the forest. The Skete had no church as such. A large room in one of the dwellings served the purpose. The community was small, and most of the monks were on in years, but they performed the Services with fervor and piety. These monks had come from their original and large monastery of Konevetz, on the island of Konevetza, in the Lake of Ladoga, the largest lake in Europe. The island was occupied by the Red Army during the Second World War. The monks took away with them only the most necessary and holy things in their hasty evacuation. Their life now in Konevitsa was simple and very poor.

Father Dorofey was well over sixty when I first met him, but he looked young and strong. And he was full of joy. As the saying has it: the soul united to God is always radiant. He came to Valaam in the beginning of the century as a very young man. Professed in Valaam, he was sent to Konevitsa later on. The community there had begun to diminish after the First World War, when it was cut of from its recruiting grounds in Russia. The Orthodox in Finland were too few to maintain two large monasteries. It was with a certain eargerness that I consulted this wise old monk from Holy Russia who had lived through the painful transition period and could still smile radiantly.

"Your Konevitsa, Father Dorofey, reminds me much of the Skete of Saint Nilos of Soza. The same solitude, the same silence, the same peace."

"Have you read, Brother Sergius, the *Tradition of Sketic Life of Saint Nilos?*"

"Yes, I have, Father. It was sent to me from Mount Athos a long time ago."

"That is good. You should read the *Tradition* frequently and meditate on it. Its contents cannot be understood at once, but they reveal themselves gradually, according to your spiritual growth. The *Sketic Tradition* is useful for all those who practice the Prayer of Jesus, especially its teaching on how to distinguish good thoughts from dangerous ones. If you fail in this, your progress in prayer will be slow, hardly possible."

"Could you summarize the teaching of Saint Nilos for me, Father? Because in the *Philokalia* and even in the *Tradition* there are many repetitions and many things that are not clear."

"Certainly. Saint Nilos did not write a textbook, and what he wrote he wrote in the style of his age. Nevertheless, it is not difficult to summarize his teaching. The saint begins with *prilog*, that is, an idea or an image, which appears in our mind or heart. This thought might be suggested by the devil, who incites us to do one thing or another. This *prilog* might be sinless in itself; then it merits neither blame nor praise. We cannot avoid having thoughts passing continually through our minds, even undesirable ones. Only those who have attained to great holiness can do so, and even they can do it only for a time, as Saint Isaac the Syrian teaches us.

"The next stage, called *connection* by the Fathers of the Desert, is our discussion with the appearing thought. This discussion might be passionate or passionless. We make *connection* when we retain the suggestion of the devil, fall in with it, and allow it to stay with us by our own choice. This the Fathers do not consider blameless, but in the end it might work out for the glory of God. This comes about when the monk, although he does not resist the sinful suggestion but discusses it within himself to the extent that the devil starts to make other suggestions, nevertheless comes to his senses and opposes the evil suggestion with a good one. For example, the devil suggests that I drink a glass of vodka. I accept this suggestion and come to the conclusion that in such bad weather to drink a glass of vodka would not only be pleasant but also very useful for my health to avoid the flu. But, immediately, I counter the suggestion with another thought. Although it would certainly be pleasant and perhaps healthful to drink a glass of vodka in this raw weather, I would be tempted to drink another glass, and a third, and gradually form a habit of drinking and become an alcoholic, with all its accompanying misery. The evil suggestion leads me to think of the virtue of sobriety, and I reject the evil proposal.

"The third stage is called by Saint Nilos *fusion.* This takes place when we accept the evil thought or image and enter into dialogue with it mentally and finally decide to do what the thought urges us to do. When an experienced monk who knows how to resist temptation and has been honored with divine assistance in the past, by neglect or laziness allows this *fusion* to take place, it is sinful. The case is different for novices and weak people. If they accept the suggestion, but soon after repent and confess their sin before the Lord and invoke his assistance, God readily forgives them in his mercy. Their kind of fusion can be easily understood and forgiven. They were overpowered mentally by the devilish suggestion, but in the depth of their hearts they preserved their attachment to God. Therefore, since sin was unrealized in the act, their union with him remained unbroken.

"The second kind of *fusion,* according to Saint Gregory of Sinai, is this: We accept devilish suggestions by our free will. We are overcome to such a degree that we cease to resist them, and decide to satisfy our passion at the first opportunity. If we do not act at once, it is only because we lack the opportunity. Such a state of soul is very sinful. This happens, for example, when one decides to fornicate but remains physically chaste because he lacks the opportunity, but he will fornicate once there is an opportunity.

"This next stage is *imprisonment*. Our heart is irresistibly attracted to the seducing thought. We retain it within us. We carry on a mental discussion with the idea, which disturbs our whole spiritual life. This happens, for example, in the case of vengeance. *Imprisonment* also has two degrees: the first, when our mind is overpowered by some idea and our thoughts turn continually to the devilish suggestion. Still we are able, with divine assistance, to turn our mind from wandering about and call it back to its business. The second is when our mind is overwhelmed as by a tempest. We find it impossible to return to our former quiet and peace. This results from worldly distractions and too much idle talk. We see here how important it is to keep silence.

"Our sinfulness is measured by the way we are overpowered: whether this happens during prayer in church or in private, whether the obsessive idea is passionate or not, whether it is indifferent or truly sinful. When devilish temptations are entertained during prayer, when our minds should be turned to God and be free of outside thoughts, this is very sinful. But when worldly thoughts come upon us outside of prayer time, this is natural enough. If these thoughts are simple and permissible and our mind remains generally concentrated, everything is all right.

"For the Fathers, passion is an inclination of the soul that is fostered so long that it becomes a habit, almost part of our nature. We arrive at this by our own free will and desire. The obsessive and sinful idea becomes rooted firmly within us, because we continually mull over it, nourish and cultivate it in our heart. Thus it becomes a habit and continually disturbs us with its passionate suggestions coming from the devil. Our foe then unceasingly pictures before us some object or some person and urges us to an exclusive love of it. Against our will, we are overpowered and become slaves to that person or thing. This leads to a neglect of prayer and a continuous preoccupation with the object. Thus a drunkard continually thinks of when and how he can obtain his drink, the fornicator is obsessed with women, the worrisome person with his money, and so on.

"Every passion must be purged away by penance in this life equal to its gravity. Otherwise we must suffer for it in the world to come. Also, we must repent and pray or we will be punished for our lack of repentance. Those who have been overpowered by passion must struggle against it and avoid all occasions that could revive it. For example, those who are vengeful must avoid the places where their offenders reside; those who are tempted to unchastity must avoid the persons who excite them, and so forth. Those who neglect the necessary precautions kill their foes or seduce the women they want first in their imagination; then, in due course, they commit the crime in fact. The ancient Fathers teach us that we must withstand passion boldly. Ultimately, we shall triumph or we shall be defeated in our mind. He who vanquishes the foe will receive the crown, while he who is defeated will endure eternal punishment. The best method to fight evil suggestions is to cut off the very first *prilog* and to practice unceasing prayer. You see, all this is quite simple," Father Dorofey finished with a big smile.

"Is all this confirmed by your experience, Father?"

"Certainly; I saw this myself in Valaam. In the old days, quite a few drunkards were sent from St. Petersburg to Valaam to be healed. They were habitual drunkards, mostly from wealthy business families. They usually remained in Valaam for three years. Valaam was an island, and its only inhabitants were monks. There were no taverns, nowhere to find vodka. Drunkards were usually employed as laborers and expected to do hard work. Church Services, work, and talks with the Spiritual Father — that was the program. A good many were completely cured within the three years, becoming teetotalers. Vodka became repulsive to them.

"The same thing happens to fornicators. We once had a young monk, about forty years of age, very handsome. He used to travel on monastic business. Well, one day he met a young teacher, lost his head, and decided to ask for secularization in order to marry her. No one could reason with him, neither the Hegumen nor the Staretz. Passion had completely overpowered him. Yet, a simple layman, a tailor, healed him. The monk had gone to him to order his lay clothes. The tailor asked him: 'Why do you need lay clothes?'

" 'I want to marry.'

" 'Whom?'

" 'Miss So-and-so.'

" 'Well,' the tailor answered. 'I know the girl. But she is not for you.'

" 'Why?'

" 'You are twenty years older than she. You are very handsome dressed as a monk. But when you are clean-shaven and dressed like a layman, you will look very different. She will quickly lose interest in you and will leave you for a younger man. She is attractive and there will be many competitors. You will break your vows for nothing and lose everything, and involve her in a lot of trouble, too. Do not listen to this devilish suggestion. Go back to Valaam and remain there for three years, going nowhere. Stay in a skete where laymen are not even allowed to visit. All your foolish imaginings will disappear in due course, quicker than you think.'

"Well, the tailor was right. The hieromonk did as the tailor suggested and came to himself, and always thanked the wise tailor for his friendly advice."

*　　*　　*

A few days later, Father Dorofey visited me in my log cabin. The sun was setting. Its golden rays shone on the giant trees and on the tranquil lake. The profound silence of the Far North reigned supreme. A red sanctuary lamp flickered before the icon in the corner honoring a Presence. I was reading the *Tradition of Sketic Life*, by Saint Nilos of Soza.

"Are you reading Saint Nilos of Soza?" asked Father Dorofey. "Read him with care and try to apply his words to your own life."

"Well, Father Dorofey, I read here that any idea coming to us in prayer time, even a good one, should be rejected at once, because it distracts us from our prayer. On the other hand, if a thought comes to us outside the time of prayer, we must cut it off at once if it is sinful, while other thoughts should be admitted only after due consideration, because bad thoughts often accompany a good idea. Is that not so?"

"Exactly. We must examine the thoughts coming to us. If an idea comes to us and appears to be a good one, yet we feel some uncertainty and hesitation about it, we must reject such a thought and look into the depths of our heart and say: 'Lord Jesus Christ, Son of God have mercy on me, a sinner.' This prayer can be varied. We may say the first half at one time, 'Lord Jesus Christ, have mercy on me, a sinner.' This prayer should be said slowly, standing, sitting, or lying down. We must enclose our mind in our heart and breathe slowly; deep, slow breathing is very useful for the concentration of our mind during prayer. Experience will quickly teach you that."

"But, Father Dorofey, if my attention is still dispersed, what should I do?"

"When we cannot pray in the solitude of the heart, that is, without outside thoughts, and when the latter grow and multiply, we must not lose courage but persevere in our prayer. Saint Gregory of Sinai said that no beginner is able to keep his attention concentrated and free of alien thoughts without extraordinary help from God. Only very spiritual and experienced persons are able to remain attentive and withstand the invasion of thoughts, and then not by their own strength but by God's grace.

"Therefore, my brother in Christ, when alien thoughts, especially impure suggestions, come to you, take no notice of them, but, reducing your breathing and shutting up your mind in your heart, continue to call on the Lord Jesus. If even then attention cannot be attained, we must pray against those very thoughts to be saved from them. If even this is of no avail, we must pray out loud, pronouncing the words slowly, patiently, and firmly. If we feel ourselves weakening or in despair, we must still call on God, asking for his help and never giving up prayer. If we are firm, temptation will vanish. Experience teaches us this.

"When our serenity is restored and we free ourselves from the overpowering and obsessing idea, we must again go back to silent prayers. Solitude is the exclusion during prayer of all alien thoughts, even those that seem good to us. To keep the mind in the heart, excluding all foreign ideas while praying, is hard work until we form the habit and experience the sweetness of prayer in the heart by the action of Divine Grace. Many people give up prayer because of their weakness and impatience, expecting quick results. Those who are overshadowed by grace pray easily and with love. Their prayer is sweet and free from captivating ideas."

"What can you say, Father Dorofey, about the hesychast method of prayer?"

"You mean, my friend, the prayer described in the *Philokalia*? This method is of secondary importance. We can learn how to pray well without this method. It is true, of course, that deep and rhythmic breathing helps to concentrate our attention. But it is merely a method. People are advised to sit on a low chair, inclining their head and neck, concentrating their mind in their heart, and then say the Prayer. It means simply that we must pray attentively and feelingly. When our mind becomes tired from the effort of this exercise and the heart feels pain on account of the unceasing calling on Christ, we start singing psalms in order to have a change.

"Yet if prayer is sweet we should not leave it to sing psalms. In order to avoid spiritual illusions while praying, we should not entertain any pictorial representations in our mind, though they will come even when our mind remains in our heart; this is, when we pray with attention and feeling. Only those illuminated by the Holy Spirit are able to keep their mind unmoved, free from all thoughts and images. True unceasing prayer is a state in which we persevere at all times in the adoration of God. This adoration is free from words and images."

"When we are praying, must we reject not only visions and voices but also abstract philosophical speculations?" I asked Father Dorofey.

"Yes. Saint Nilos believed that those who do not practice the Prayer of Jesus, which is the source of many virtues and of spiritual joy, should sing and read psalms in the Services often and at length. However, those who have progressed well and are filled with the Grace of the Holy Spirit do not need long Services but, rather, the silence of unceasing prayer and contemplation. Of course, this is more suitable for hermits than for those living in communities. The solitaries, when they are united to the Lord in their Prayer, must not leave their conversation with him and be confused by vocal prayers."

"What do you think, Father Dorofey, of this quotation from Isaac the Syrian which I have copied:

Those who have experienced this spiritual and desirable joy know that this suddenly puts a stop to vocal prayer because the lips, then the tongue, the heart — treasurer of thoughts — and the mind —

guide of feelings and thought — cease to act. Then the mind has no more prayer, but is moved on by another force, not its own. The mind is mysteriously captured and experiences something indescribable. This state is called "ecstasy" or the "vision of prayer." This is no longer prayer, properly speaking, because the mind is above prayer and has no desire. The soul of the ascetic now enters into an incomprehensible union, becoming truly God-like. It is illuminated in all its movements by the ray of Eternal Light. The mind begins to experience something of the future beatitude. It forgets itself and everything transitory, everything earthly. There is no more prayer, no matter how pure. The soul is filled with indescribable joy, the heart overflowing with transcendent sweetness, which penetrates the very body. Man then forgets all merely human passions and even his very life, and is certain that the Kingdom of Heaven is nothing more than the state in which he is.

"What do you say of this?"

"My dear Brother Sergius, of such things they alone can speak who have experienced them personally. If you have had such experience in any degree, you should consult Father Michael at Uusi Valamo. He has been both a hermit and a recluse and has had much experience. Personally, I may only repeat the words spoken by Saint Pimen the Great to a pilgrim who asked him about many things, spiritual and transcendent. At first, Abba Pimen answered not a word. When he was asked why he remained silent, he replied: 'If I were asked about passions and sins and how to heal them I would reply with joy, but this pilgrim asks me about spiritual things, which are unknown to me.' When the visitor asked Saint Pimen how to fight passions and to avoid sins, the Egyptian ascetic became happy and said: 'Now I shall open my mouth.' "

I had many talks with Father Dorofey during my stay in the little log cabin at the edge of the forest. Finally, on the day of my departure, after Liturgy and lunch, we walked once more together along the shore of the lake. It was a warm, sunny day. Wild geese were circling in the air above the lake. The blue line of distant forests blocked the horizon. The little skete stood silent, immersed in serenity and prayer, like one of the pictures of Nesterov or Levitan. A horse-drawn carriage was standing before my log cabin.

Father Dorofey blessed me. The horse started to trot. I looked for the last time toward the little log cabin, Father Dorofey, and the lake beyond. The horse started to run. We went through a thick and fine forest toward the highroad, where a coach was to take me to Kuoius. I was on my way to Uusi Valamo.

In the Far North

Hieromonk John of Petchenga

When I think of Father John, there comes to my mind that wonderful summer evening in Uusi Konevitsa, in Finland. The rays of the sun shine in upon the altar. Father John stands before it, presiding at the Vesper Service. His golden phelonion* is like a living flame, and his face, too, shines as though illumined from within.

I stand in a corner of the sanctuary. From the open window, I see the cloudless blue sky, the still, broad lake, and the endless forests. The Service progresses slowly. The monks sing unhurriedly. Everywhere there is peace, an atmosphere of deep, pervading silence. The Holy Mother of God looks down upon us from the ancient icon of Our Lady of Konevetz, brought by Saint Ayeny from Mount Athos in 1393.

Father John had been ordained a priest only a short time before we met. He had begun his monastic life in the monastery of Saint Arthemy of Vervholsk, one of the most attractive monasteries of the Far North, on the river Pinega, four hundred kilometers from Arkhangelsk, on the White Sea. This monastery is surrounded by impenetrable forests, tundras, and marshlands. Roads and even footpaths are rare. It is a true solitude.

Anyone who visits Vervholsk Monastery is greatly impressed by its surroundings. Without any difficulty, the visitor forgets the world of teeming cities, vanities of all sorts, and much unhappiness. His soul is immersed in a quiet yet luminous contemplation of a nature perpetually wrapped in winter and its solemn stillness. The vanity of a worldly life, the unavoidable reality of death, readily come to mind. And yet these thoughts cause no depression, but, rather, a peculiar joy, one that is quiet and a little sad. The visitor, far removed from all earthly distractions and temptations, cannot but think of his interior life and of its need to be reinvigorated. According to the monastic saying, "Church and cell will teach you how to live and what to do."

Sometime after his tonsure, Father John was invited to Saint Trifon Monastery, at Petchenga, on the Russo-Norwegian border, far beyond the Arctic Circle. Surprisingly, because of the nearness of the Atlantic Ocean and the warm current of the Gulf Stream, the climate of Petchenga is mild for such a high latitude. The average winter temperature is only six degrees below zero Celsius and frosts fifteen degrees below are very rare. Spring begins at the end of April at Petchenga, after a month of rain and fog; numberless migratory birds come to the tundras, and the fishing season begins. In May the rivers become free of ice.

The summer season begins in July and lasts two months. The average temperature is only eight degrees Celsius, but it may rise to twenty-two degrees. The weather is warm and still. Nowhere in the world does the forest come so far to the north as in Petchenga. These arctic forests are silent. There are many birds, but they do not sing. And there are many flowers. The long, warm, silent days of summer have their own special charm. The sun shines all twenty-four hours and the blue sky is cloudless. Because of the purity of the air, the distant mountains are clearly and sharply visible.

Autumn, like spring, is rainy and foggy. Winter returns early in November, and on December 9, the sun disappears, to show itself again only on the fourth of February. Nevertheless, the polar night is not a continuous darkness, and unrelieved gloom. The white snow gives some relief. And when the aurora borealis begins to play, which it does frequently, it is bright enough to read with ease. There are, too, wonderful starry displays and floods of moonlight. At the beginning and at the end of the long night there are sunrises and sunsets that color the horizon for hours even though the sun does not appear.

On the whole, the climate of Petchenga is healthful and the local inhabitants have a reputation for longevity.

In my childhood I knew people who visited the Skete of Saint

Nicholas, the northernmost monastery of the Russian Empire, situated near the settlement of Malyye Karmakuly, on the island of Novaya Zemlya, in the Arctic Ocean. Novaya Zemlya reminds one of New Zealand, in the Pacific Ocean. It is about the same size and is really two islands separated by narrow straits. Novaya Zemlya is about fifteen hundred kilometers long and four hundred kilometers wide. Its terrain and climate are exceedingly rugged. The island itself is a conglomeration of rocks and stones. Snow lies in the mountains nearly all year round. And there are ice fields. The arctic night in Novaya is longer than in Petchenga.

The average winter temperature is twelve degrees below zero. Both in autumn and winter the aurora borealis is very active. At the end of March, sunrise and sunset meet, and on May 17, the arctic day begins. The sun remains continuously in the sky and nature awakes rapidly. Already in the beginning of June the grass comes up. However, even in summer the temperature never rises above fifteen degrees.

The inhabitants of Novaya Zemlya are Samoyeds, or Samya, cousins of the Eskimos of Greenland, Siberia, and North America. They were settled on the island by the Russian Imperial Government in 1848. Previously the island had been quite empty. The Skete of Saint Nicholas was a missionary venture. It disappeared during the revolution. Khrushchev used Novaya Zemlya as the testing ground for the most destructive hydrogen bombs and was appalled by the results. Compared with Novaya Zemlya, the neighboring Petchenga seems almost semitropical.

While the Skete of Saint Nicholas was a recent foundation, Petchenga Monastery was not. It was founded in 1533 by Saint Triphon, who evangelized the Laplanders. In 1590, on Christmas Day, Swedish pirates attacked the monastery, killed all the monks looted the church, and burned all the buildings. The surviving monks — those who were absent from the monastery during the massacre — moved to Kola, in the eastern part of Russian Lapland, and founded a new monastery there. Only in 1886 was Petchenga Monastery restored, and it developed very rapidly. In the beginning of the present century there were about fifty professed monks and one hundred fifty novices, postulants, and oblates.

In 1920 the Soviet Government surrendered to Finland the small district in which Petchenga Monastery was situated. In this way Petchenga escaped the fate of other Russian monasteries: suppressed by the Soviet Government. Just before the Second World War there were still twenty monks in the monastery, all of them from Russia's Far North. During the last war, the monks were evacuated to Konevitsa, where I found the few survivors.

The Far North always reminds me of that joyous and yet slightly sad state of mind described as *radosto-pechalie*; for want of better words, "joyfully sad." All the beauty of those endless forests and numberless lakes, still and deep, I appreciated in Konevitsa. The Far North, more than any other place on earth, gives one the impression of the nearness of the invisible city of God.

Father John was, like a true son of the Far North, *radosto-pechalie* — joyous, calm, contemplative. He was not a great talker, immersed as he was in prayer and contemplation. Once, I asked him: "Father, tell me, is it true that in order to be 'saved,' to 'live in God,' we must live away from crowds, as you do here in the North?"

He answered: "I believe it is true, man of God. It is very difficult to lead a holy life in the world. There is so much activity and so much vanity. When the devil wants to detach someone from the one thing necessary, he occupies him with a lot of work which does not leave him a free moment for meditation or for deepening his interior life. As a result, the prayer of one who lives in the world is full of distractions, dry, and tedious. He may even give up prayer altogether. Such a man is 'drowned' in the world. Of course, men can be saved in the world, but it is so much more difficult. The early monks went to the desert in order to be alone with God. It is very difficult indeed to serve God and the world at the same time, but such is unavoidable when one lives in the world."

I asked if the Prayer of Jesus could not assist such a one. Father replied that it could, but in order to practice the Prayer seriously one really needs solitude, silence, and concentration. These are hardly attainable in the world, with its vanities, noises, and passions, which blind men and push them into sins and crimes. Blessed is the man whom the Lord calls to live and to pray to him in these northern forests. When the Kingdom of God comes, all "practical" activities will

disappear. The only occupation of the blessed will be unceasing praise
of the glory of God, as is that of the angels and saints even now in
heaven before the throne of God.

I told Father John how I lived for a while in the province of
Nizhny Novgorod, where Lake Svetly Gar is situated and with which
the legend of the City of Kitiesh is associated. People are strongly
aware of an invisible presence at Lake Svetly Gar. Now I felt this even
more strongly at Uusi Konevitsa. I asked Father if people did not feel
this even more in Petchenga or in Novaya Zemlya.

"The invisible world, Sergei Nikolaevich," he answered, "sur-
rounds us everywhere, but it is easier to sense its presence when we are
in solitude than among crowds."

I remembered and spoke to Father about one night many years
before when I was traveling in the Far North. The absolute stillness of
that night, with its myriad of brilliant stars, overawed me. And then
the incredibly beautiful aurora borealis began to display its arches and
curtains of all colors, hovering over and illuminating the pure white
snow. It was like entering into the invisible world of eternity, where
there is neither time nor space.

"Yes, I believe I did."

"Well, then, blessed are you, my dear friend. You are on the right
path. You may suffer, you may hesitate, but you will move in the right
direction. True wisdom is very simple. Always keep your peace of
mind. You can do that only by accepting everything God sends you
and not wishing for anything else. Father Theophan of the Pskovo-
Petchersky Monastery told me this: If we meditate seriously on our
life, we readily see how the hand of God has led us through even the
most difficult circumstances. It is only an experience such as this that
makes our faith solid as a rock. The speculations of the rationalists and
the wise ones of this world lead us nowhere and may very well destroy
our faith."

As the time for my departure was drawing near, I asked Father
John for a word of life: "Father," I said, "I shall soon be leaving the
Northland, the gateway to the invisible city of God. What instruction
would you offer me?"

Father said very simply: "The invisible city — as you yourself
declared, speaking of Kitiesh — is our heart. We must retire there for

prayer and meditation. At first we can manage to do this only from time to time, but with practice we will be able to abide there continually."

This seemed impossible to me, so I objected: "But, to do that, one must retire to a remote monastery or skete. How could one do such a thing in the world?"

"One can," replied the holy monk. "Father John of Kronstadt, a saintly priest and preacher, my fellow countryman from the province of Arkhangelsk, lived a most strenuous active life and yet he was a great man of prayer and contemplation. It is difficult, but not impossible. As you practice the Prayer of Jesus, say it slowly and patiently. Do not hurry, as many do, for that comes to nothing. Time itself will bring results: peace of mind and detachment. You will find then that you have indeed mastered yourself.

"And there is something else that it is important to observe: Avoid noise and publicity. Do your work in such a way that your left hand does not know what your right hand is doing. Do not run after people. You will not find either security or justice in them, but only in God. To enter the invisible city, you must be pure of heart, as it is justly said of those who wish to enter Kitiesh. For such purity of heart all of us must strive, Sergei Nikolaevich. May God lead us both in this way. Amen."

Hegumen John

Exiled from Solitude

In August 1954 I was in Uusi Valamo, in Finland. In the course of my visit I had several long talks with Father John. He was at that time confessor of the community. He had been Hegumen of Petchenga.

In particular I remember one afternoon, still and sunny. One sensed already the approach of the long, northern winter, although it was only the second half of August. The air was clear and pure, free of all pollution. The shadows were sharp and the water in the lake pale blue. Light, white cloudlets chased each other across a pale blue sky. The wonderful silence of the North reigned around us. This was truly a spot for prayer and meditation, far away from the crowds, noise, and dirt of the teeming cities.

I greeted the Hegumen and received his blessing. "It is very fine here, Father John. It is so quiet and so remote."

"This is nothing compared to Petchenga," answered the monk.

Petchenga is truly remote. In winter it is totally isolated. Nothing but the snow-covered tundra, and the distant roar of the ocean in the background. This is the case even now. But what it was in the sixteenth century, when Saint Triphon, the Apostle of the Lapps, first arrived there and founded the monastery, is beyond description. In those days Petchenga was indeed remote.

Saint Seraphim of Sarov used to say, "Solitude, prayer, charity, and abstinence are the four wheels of the chariot that carries the spirit to heaven." In Petchenga one has every opportunity to practice these four virtues. Solitude is indeed present; there are no human habitations for miles. Solitude, with its silence, promotes true prayer, undistracted, attentive, sober. There is every opportunity to practice charity, for the Lapps come from time to time to the monastery either to pray or to ask for something. Finally, in the rude conditions of the tundra, with its cold and darkness, and its sterility, one may practice abstinence to his heart's content.

I told the Hegumen how I once lived for a time in the Russian North. I loved it: the great silence, especially at night, the wonderful aurora borealis, the starry skies, the virgin snow, and the great, dark forest. But the tundra I always found depressing.

Father John agreed. In the Far North only really good monks can survive, those with the true prayer of the heart. In the milder climates, there are many pleasing distractions: the change of seasons, the flowers, singing birds, wild beasts. But not so the Far North: there is the monotonous, nine-month-long winter with a night that lasts three months, and then a short and rather hot summer when the tundra turns into an immense marshy land with clouds of mosquitoes that torment men and animals without respite. Only perfectly balanced men with true peace of mind who are able to pray and meditate continuously can survive. They are helped by the fact that there is manual work and plenty of it. Orchards, fishing, the herds of reindeer, and so on.

I had recently met a scientist who spent several years in Antarctica, where the climatic conditions are worse than in Petchenga or even in Novaya Zemlya, the skete beyond the Arctic Circle. He was working with a scientific expedition. They lived in houses under the snow. Although rude and simple, these houses were quite comfortable and well heated. They allowed the men to persevere in their scientific observations and experiments. I asked him whether he liked Antarctica and whether he would like to return. To my astonishment he said that he like it greatly and would not mind returning to it. The great attraction of Antarctica, this scientist said, lay in its incomparable silence and solitude. The air is pure and invigorating. There is no smoke from factory chimneys, no exhaust fumes from cars, no noise. During the day the blinding white of the snow and the blue sky, and at night the incomparably starry sky and the display of the wonderful aurora australis. And there is also life, especially along the coast:

crowds of funny penguins, all kinds of birds, whales and other sea creatures. In Antarctica one naturally tends to live in astonishment before the grandeur of the cosmos and to meditate on the indescribable power and wisdom of God. I asked this scientist whether religious life is possible in Antarctica or not. "Why not?" he answered. "If scientists can live there, the monks can live there too, and more easily because they are more accustomed to live an interior life. Of course, they must have some occupation; they could conduct scientific observations and experiments."

When I stayed two years ago in Boquen Abbey, in Brittany, its founder, my old friend Abbot Alexis Presse, told me about the celebrated French scientist and Nobel prizewinner Alexis Carrel. At the end of his life, Carrel returned to the Christian faith after years in the religious wilderness. This scientist had dreamed of the foundation of a religious community that would support itself not by agriculture or industry but by scientific research. I asked the Hegumen if he thought such a thing might be possible.

"Why not? Every work done for God or neighbor is good. Scientific research is good, if pursued with humility."

I went on to ask Father John why Russian monks always moved toward the North. It was his conviction that they started to move from the Kiev area to the North after the Mongol invasion had devastated the country there and everyone felt insecure. Religious life, if properly lived, demands solitude, peace, and silence. What peace could there be if raiders could be expected to arrive at any moment to kill and loot? But the Mongols could not penetrate the great northern forests. There was nothing to loot there. In the North, there was security. So the monks moved to the North, always farther and farther, till at length they crossed the Arctic Circle. Of course, perfect security is not of this world. Even Petchenga was looted from time to time by Scandinavian pirates and Lapp marauders. The same happened to Valaam, but Solovki was so remote and so inaccessible that it remained intact until the Bolshevik Revolution, when it was turned into a prison.

I wondered if now, when the world is so quickly filling up and solitude is harder and harder to find, the same trend might not begin again. Father thought it quite possible. Those who really love solitude can find it at its best in the polar region, remote, harsh, and barely accessible. But even there one must live quietly; otherwise the curious will come. They started to flock even to Petchenga in the last years before the Second World War. Still, we must always remember that the most important solitude is the inner solitude.

"What is inner solitude?" I asked. And Father John replied most beautifully. "Inner solitude is God and the soul, nothing more." What benefit is it for us to dwell in external solitude if we have our minds continually occupied with worldly thoughts and passions? Distractions and vain, wandering thoughts come because in our innermost selves we do not believe in the presence of God everywhere. He whose thoughts wander about even in church can hardly be called a devout Christian. All our troubles come about because of the absence within us of the fear of God. The Far North is a good teacher of the fear of God. In those endless snow-covered plains, where there is no town or village, we are confronted with eternal and unchangeable facts. The night sky, clear and dark, is lit up with myriads of stars and the mysterious aurora borealis. Father asked me if I had seen this magnificent phenomenon.

Yes I had, many times. It is an awe-inspiring spectacle: the many colored arches, curtains, and cascades, all silent and beautiful. In the face of such splendor one feels so small, puny, utterly insignificant.

"There, my dear Sergei Nikolaevich, is the beginning of the fear of God, this sentiment or sensation of the utter nothingness of oneself and of the incomprehensible power and glory of God." Father went on to point out that, in the towns, we hardly see nature. We are surrounded on all sides with the man-made wonders of technology. But how insignificant they are seen to be when compared with the bottomless abysses of the God of creation! Living among man-made things makes us proud and arrogant. Man begins to believe he is the master of the universe, a genius leading a brute and unthinking nature to perfection. This is a dangerous illusion, similar to that of Satan. Man wants to be God, but he is not. He is merely a very insignificant creature lost in the enormous spaces of the cosmos. Father said he often meditated on this when he was in Petchenga.

"It would be fine to found a monastery in the Far North, Father, like your Petchenga or the Skete of Novaya Zemlya," I mused.

"Yes," he agreed, "it would be, but for the time being it is hardly possible." He went on to explain that they could not found a monastery in Finnish Lapland, because they were so few and old. Since the Soviet troops occupied Petchenga, the little community has been in exile. Some were in Uusi Konevitsa and some were at Uusi Valamo. Uusi Konevitsa had so few monks that it, itself, was on the point of disappearing. Father expected the surviving monks would join the little group at Uusi Valamo. And then the end of Uusi Valamo itself would be near. It seemed to be but a question of time. The Orthodox Church of Finland has hardly more than seventy thousand people, and it is unable to maintain three monasteries. Moreover, the spirit of its clergy is far from favoring the monastic. No monastery could be founded in the Soviet North, which stretches from Finland to Alaska.

"Perhaps one could be founded in Alaska or Canada," I conjectured. Father doubted this. There were nearly five million Orthodox in North America, of many ethnic origins, with the Greeks forming the largest group. But the monastic spirit was absent. The Greeks have been unable to found a single monastery of their own. The Russians of the Metropolia* have Saint Tikhon's Monastery in Pennsylvania, but it is not a flourishing community. The Russian traditionalists have a good monastery in Jordanville, New York, but it is very "active," not "contemplative," and in the Far North only the latter would do. (The flourishing skete that exists in Boston today was not yet in existence.) Still, Father hoped it might happen one day. A movement is on foot to canonize the Valaam Staretz Germanus, who died in 1837 in Alaska. The Alaskan mission was founded by the Valaam community at the end of the eighteenth century.

I then asked, "Could hermits exist in the Far North, Father?"

"I doubt this very much," he replied. "Life in those frozen tundras is very harsh indeed. The cold is intense and it lasts many months. Houses must be well heated in order simply to survive, and food must be plentiful and nourishing. And then there is the great northern loneliness. It might well bring on deep melancholy. Father Jonah told me that. He had come from Valaam, where there was a large community, a beautiful view, a great lake, fine forests with a lot of animals. In Petchenga he found the endless tundra and the long nights monotonous and depressing." Father John went on: It is hard to live in a small community cheek by jowl. It is perhaps harder than to live alone. Only monks with a deep and settled interior life should go to the Far North, those for whom only God matters. For them the Far North is a true paradise. One rapidly acquires the fear of God, a sense of awe and adoration, while contemplating a starry sky, the aurora borealis, or the frightful storms in the glacial ocean. And the fear of God is the beginning of all wisdom. Naturally it is easier to acquire in the Far North continuous prayer of the heart. There are no distractions. Attention is easily concentrated. One really needs to experience all this for oneself.

Father went on, speaking softly and slowly: God is within us. In the world, because our attention is continually dispersed, it takes a long time to find him. In the Far North it is easy. Indeed the Far North is the same desert as that of the Egyptian hermits, except it is covered with snow. In the Far North, the continuous prayer is very restful, because it saves us from daydreaming, something very common when life is monotonous. Daydreaming usually leads to illusions, which are very dangerous in the loneliness of the Far North.

"Remember," Father said, "no one can approach God before he leaves the world."

The "world," according to the Fathers, is the totality of passions, and when they live within us we are still in the world. To purify ourselves from these passions, we must enter into our inner chamber and throw them out by prayer and ascetical living. Those who think they can master their passions, and the sins born of them, without continuous prayer and hard living delude themselves. We can save ourselves anywhere in any situation, provided we pray continually and live soberly. If we do this we can master the very devils, as Christ himself told the Apostles. The Far North merely offers a better situation in which to practice continuous prayer of the heart and abstemious living.

The bell in the tower started to ring. "It is time to go to church for Vespers," Father John said as he stood up. We went to the church.

I had another discussion with Father John on the monastic life in the Far North. It took place in the morning, after Liturgy, out by the lake. I told Father of the great Volga forests, of the skete on Kerznenets, of Staretz Zosima Verkhovsky, elements of whose life were used by Dostoevski in his *Brothers Karamazov* to depict Staretz Zosima.

Many people, Father John said wisely, have romantic ideas about monastic life and the Far North. That is not good. When they meet the hard realities of life, they become despondent and unhappy. In life we must never set our hearts on any kind of blessedness. That awaits us in the world to come. We must, on the contrary, look on our life as the way of the cross, as a merited penance for our sins. The Fathers say: "Pray well and expect the worst." It is obvious, the more progress we make in prayer and ascetical living the more excited the devil becomes and he plays all kinds of tricks on us.

I asked a final question: "How can we find our way in life, Father?"

"The very circumstances of our life show us the way; also the advice of God-fearing people and the intimations of our religious superiors. We must never follow our own inclinations and choose the things that appear to us best and most desirable. It is here that danger lies in wait for us. If you would go to the Far North to satisfy your fancy, then do not go; but if you are sent, then, indeed, do go. I was sent to Petchenga. It was my duty to go."

It is these very simple and humble words that have remained with me as the fruit of my encounter with Father John of Petchenga.

The Tradition of Valaam

Hieroschimonk Luke

I arrived at Uusi Valamo, in southern Finland, on August 9, 1954, on a steamer from Kuopio. Uusi Valamo is at the same latitude as southern Greenland, Alaska, and northern Kamchatka, Siberia. Our small boat nosed its way through the bewildering succession of lakes of northern Saimaa. The farther we moved to the northeast the wilder and emptier the country became. Tall and silent forests lined the shore of the lakes through which we were passing. Hardly any dwellings or fields were to be seen. The region is all forest, bathed in solitude and silence. After the hurried, restless, and unhappy life of teeming cities, this grandiose temple of God was a revelation. In this world of vast distances and solitude, city life seemed petty and unreal.

At four o'clock in the afternoon the steamer entered a small and charming lake with a miniature harbor. We had arrived at Uusi Valamo. In 1954 the monastery housed a community of seventy-five monks who had arrived in 1940 from the celebrated Valaam, on the islands of the Lake of Ladoga, which had been occupied by the Soviet troops. Since their arrival, the monks have lived in the scattered houses of the country estate they bought and adapted to their requirements. I remained for a relatively short time in Uusi Valamo, but I discussed many things with the monks and learned much.

Father Luke, guestmaster of Uusi Valamo, was not only very friendly but also deeply spiritual. He had been guestmaster for many years while the community was still in Valaam. He knew well how to deal with people and what to say. I spoke with him chiefly about the monastic tradition of Valaam. One day, I asked him what the celebrated Hegumen of Valaam, Staretz Nazary, used to teach about prayer. In response he gave me a little book to read. I read:

> When you are standing in the church and you cannot hear well what is sung or read, then say devoutly the Prayer of Jesus. Try your best to implant this Prayer firmly in your soul and heart. Say the Prayer in your mind. Do not allow it to leave your lips. Unite it with your breathing. Bring yourself to heartfelt sorrow and, if you are able, to tears. Do this always. Keep silence and restrain your mind from distractions and artful and cunning thoughts. Persevere always in this way with humility and penance, waiting till Divine Grace overshadows and illumines you. When you leave the church to go to your cell, continue to say the Prayer of Jesus. And in your cell go on with the Jesus Prayer, using your prayer cord.* Any old man, any sick person can do that. Remain in prayer and silence in your cell. When some particular manual labor is not prescribed, read or undertake some handicraft. When you leave your cell, do not engage in vain talk with the people you meet on your way. If you are able, eat only once a day. When you are serving table in the refectory, always let your face and eyes witness to a heart that is gay. When you are not serving, take one of the lower seats, if possible even the last.

When I finished the book, I returned it to Father Luke and we discussed the matter. "In this little book everything is so simple, Father Luke."

"If you live simply you will live to be a hundred," Father Luke answered. He went on to say that in the world everything is complicated and confused, but for the monk everything is simple. Anyone who practices the Prayer of Jesus must live simply, because only a simple life enables one to avoid sin. Staretz Nazary taught that we must always watch over ourselves because passion always begins with something small, hardly observable, but then grows and multiplies exceedingly. We must especially watch over our belly, because tasty and pleasant food, washed down with strong drink, leads us straight to gluttony, sensual living, and drunkenness, which in turn excite our sexuality. This is most contrary to the commitment of the monk and dangerous also for secular clergy and laity alike, because it can only lead to vice and ill health.

I told Father Luke of an Anglican clergyman who died at the age of one hundred and four and celebrated in the church on the very day of his death. When people would ask him to what he attributed his longevity, he used to keep silence, but finally he said: "I believe when we are young we may eat as much as we can. Later we should be satisfied with what is given to us, but after seventy we must eat little, and less and less every year."

Father Luke replied: "This is wise, my friend."

Bishop Isidore, Metropolitan of Novgorod, St. Petersburg, and Finland, who died in office at ninety-three, always gave this answer to those who were astonished at his age and abilities: "The secret of this health, my dear Fathers and Brothers, is simple. I was never overworried about anything. We are pilgrims, who have no abiding city but look for the world to come. We must not be attached, therefore, to anything earthly and transitory. Saint John Damascene writes in the same vein in his Office of the Dead. What worldly pleasure is free from sorrow? What glory on this earth remains unchanged? Everything is a passing shadow, a dream and an illusion. In a single moment death destroys all that."

Father Nazary was right in saying that no one who intends to lead an ascetical life can avoid sorrows and troubles, because people naturally do not want to face unchallengeable truth. They prefer to harbor the illusion that there will be no retribution for their passions and vices. They hate those whose lives condemn them. This happens even in monasteries. A monk hardly begins to lead a truly ascetical life before the devil begins to make trouble for him. Sometimes it comes from his superiors, sometimes from those who are living indifferent lives. They will start to speak of him with irony: "Look what a holy man has appeared! A hypocrite, a fool!" When this happens he must remain silent, be humble, and keep the Prayer of Jesus on the lips and in the heart. He must not become discouraged, remembering the multitude of his sins, and receive with gratitude the humiliations that heal his weaknesses.

As Father shared all this, I could not help but think and even say, "But this is hard, Father Luke."

"Who says that it is easy? With us in Valaam, those who practiced the Prayer of Jesus were advised to go to their Spiritual Father for daily confession of thoughts." Father Nazary said this:

> After the evening meal go to your Spiritual Father, bow before him, kneel, and open to him the state of your soul during the day just ended, describing all you did, in deed and in word, how you thought ill of people, how you were given to vanity and pride, how you offended your brothers or were offended by them and condemned them. Try to watch over your most insignificant thoughts, which disturb the purity and peace of your soul. If you cannot remember everything, note things down on paper. After confession and receiving absolution, which comes as it were from God himself, kiss the cross and the icon and prostrate yourself before the Staretz and then return to your cell. Continue to recite in your mind, while walking, the Prayer of Jesus, and diligently avoid all meetings and conversations in order not to be scandalized nor to scandalize others. When you reach your cell, make your thanksgiving, read for a time, and then stand up for the night vigil.

I remarked that it seemed to me that such a life is possible only in monasteries where there is a Staretz, but not in the world.

Father agreed that in the world one must have another rule. Yet with a daily confession of thoughts everything goes on much quicker. We must make progress not only in prayer but also in keeping guard over our thoughts.

Father Luke then told me that Father Nazary gave the following advice for when one prayed alone:

> First of all, lift up your mind and your heart to God and realize to whom you pray. Watch that your thoughts do not wander here and there. Lay aside your preoccupations with worldly things. After that, in deep silence and serenity of heart, stand before the icon, incline your head, cross your hands on your breast, place your feet close together, and close your eyes. Pray mentally, let the tears flow, give vent to sighs, reproach yourself. Repent, ask God to forgive all your sins, weep. Observe what psalms influence you most, bring you to deep sorrow, arouse your feelings, calling forth tears. Use those psalms often. Nevertheless, do not become anxious. It is not

important to read or to sing everything prescribed; what is important is to read or sing with feeling, tenderness, sorrow of heart. If obedience and duty call you away, go in peace. Do not feel guilty about reducing your private prayer. In old age and in sickness, pray as you can, sitting or lying down, and reproach yourself: Well, I am old now and ill. I am not able to pray as I ought and to thank God for his great mercies to me, unworthy and sick.

I had heard that they also had Staretz Agapy, who was a teacher of prayer, and inquired about him.

"Yes, he lived in Valaam and taught many monks, just as Father Nazary did." And then Father Luke went on to speak at length of Father Agapy's teaching. Perhaps with even greater insistence, Father Agapy used to say that prayer in the beginning is difficult. Only by forming ourselves through practice can we hope to acquire it. But if we have a firm resolution to become men of prayer, its practice becomes easier and easier. Finally, we become even irresistibly attracted to it. In vocal prayer we must pronounce all the words slowly, meditatively, concentrating our attention on the thoughts expressed in the words of the prayer. When our mind is distracted by alien thoughts we must return, without annoyance or depression, to the words of our prayer.

Wholeness of mind comes slowly, not when we want it but when we become humble and when God gives it to us. We attain to undistracted prayer neither by time nor by the number of prayers we say, as some people believe, but by a humble heart, by continuous effort to pray well, and by grace. Attentive vocal prayer, of itself, passes on to mental prayer. Prayer is called "mental" when we approach God with only the mind or when we contemplate God. But when we pray mentally we must keep our attention in the heart; that is, we must pray with feeling. In due course the Lord will grant us, for our humility and labor, a wholeness and concentration in prayer. When our attention to the Lord becomes continuous, it is called "attention by grace," because our own attention is always supported by God's grace.

With the help of an experienced Staretz, our mental prayer will gradually transform itself into the interior Prayer of the Heart. The Prayer of the Heart is that prayer in which we feel in our heart that we are with God and our heart is fired with love for him. He who wants to practice prayer rightly must, according to the Gospel, deny himself of his own will and human reasoning and take up the cross: endure patiently all the hardships, spiritual and bodily, that are a necessary part of the ascetical life.

"What is the place of heart, Father Luke? How does one bring about a union between mind and heart?"

Father patiently answered my questions, explaining that when an ascetic gives himself up entirely to Divine Providence and humbles himself and is ready to endure the work of prayer, the Lord God, in due course, brings to an end the man's efforts and stabilizes his mind and heart with the abiding memory of God in his heart. When such a state of mind becomes perpetual and as it were natural, this is the union of mind and heart. This is truly unceasing prayer without words or images. In this state the mind does not want to wander about, and if by business or much talking it is precluded from dwelling in the heart, it is irresistibly drawn to return to itself and to continue building the interior cell. In such a state everything in man passes on from the head to the heart, from discursive reason to intention; all leads to spiritual enlightenment.

Then an incomprehensible spiritual light illumines the ascetic and bathes all his interior in light. Everything that he thinks and does, he does now with entire consciousness and attention. It is a transfiguration. The man of prayer then sees from whence come his thoughts, intentions, desires, etc. He is able then to force his reason, heart, and will to obey Christ and to fulfill the Will of God and to carry out the command of the Father. If he transgresses, he at once redeems his fault with true penance and humbly prostrates himself before God, who has pity and continues to supply the ascetic with his grace. All this can be understood only by personal experience.

Contemplation comes when a heart is altogether purified. The ascetic then realizes his utter insignificance before God and continually sees his own sinfulness. These sentiments of poverty and unceasing penance are accompanied by a constant expectation of death, judgment, and the eternal sentence. The ascetic meditates on the life of Christ, his Passion, and his teaching as they are described in the Holy Scriptures and explained by the Fathers. Finally, he contemplates the divine attributes: divine omniscience, omnipotence, wisdom, almightiness, goodness, love of men, justice, and long-suffering.

Father Agapy corresponded with Bishop Theophan the Recluse and asked his advice. The Bishop believed that the most important thing is to live in the Presence of God, remembering him always. The Prayer of the Heart is therefore a prayer of humble sentiments or penance with the continual remembrance of the all-present God, who sees everything. This produces in us fear and piety. All the rest, such as the inclination of the head, sitting on a low chair, particular breathing, et cetera, are nothing more than methods, which add nothing essential. We may say prayers while we are walking or sitting, but in the cell it is better to pray with metanias,* or deep bows.

There is "prayer without words." This means we remain continually in prayerful sentiments toward God without pronouncing words with our lips or in our mind, and of course without any images. According to Bishop Theophan, this is the supreme degree of prayer. Only such a prayer can be unceasing.

"This is the teaching of our men of prayer. If you want to learn something more," Father Luke added, "our Staretz, Father Michael, might tell you. He has been a hermit and recluse and obtained the rare gift of tears of grace."

I met Father Luke once more, in 1960, in Pskovo-Petchersky Monastery, when I visited the Soviet Union. He then lived with Father Michael in a separate house with a chapel, the one in which I visited Father Pimen in 1926. The house is surrounded by a garden. Father Luke met me at the entrance. He was now bent with years but as friendly as before and very evidently filled with the Holy Spirit. His words were crisp: "Well, we meet again, my dear friend. You still search for spiritual wisdom? Search and you will find it. Did you visit Mount Athos? Did you see Father Ilian? A long time ago, he visited us in Valaam. I hear that he is a true Staretz now. Did you come to see Father Michael? Come along."

After my conversation with Father Michael, I said but a few words to Father Luke. I was in a hurry to return to Leningrad. Father Luke died some years later, at the age of ninety-three. Bishops, crowds of clergy, and a multitude of lay folk from Moscow, Leningrad, and even farther away came to his burial. Thus ended the witness of the last of the surviving Valaam Startzy who came with Father Michael to Pskovo-Petchersky Monastery from Finland in 1957.

The Recluse of
Uusi Valamo

Hieroschimonk Michael

I was sitting with Father Michael in his cell. The day was declining toward evening, and twilight filled the room. In the corner, before the icons, an oil lamp flickered. All was quiet and at peace. A holy light, in a spiritual silence — like the movement of angel's wings — reigns over the room.

"Tell me, Father Michael," I said, "what are the tears of grace?"

"The tears of grace, my friend, are the sign of perfect prayer and of the forgiveness of sins. Saint Isaac the Syrian writes well on this subject." Father Michael took a book from his table and handed it to me: "Read, please, the marked passages."

"Yes, Father Michael," I said. Taking the book, I started to read:

When your soul is approaching the time to leave the obscurity, this will be your sign. Your heart will begin to burn as fire, and every day and night it will burn stronger. The entire world becomes for you a cloud of dust and ashes. You do not even want to eat because of the sweet, new, fiery thoughts unceasingly awakening in your soul. Suddenly a source of tears is granted to you. It is a stream, which runs on effortlessly and mixes with all your deeds, while you are reading, praying, meditating, eating, drinking, and so on.

When you see this happening in your soul, be of good cheer, because you have crossed the sea. Keep continuous watch in order to grow daily in grace. Until you experience this state, your journey is not yet finished; you have not yet ascended the mountain of God. If, after all this, you see your tears drying up and your fire dying down without bodily sickness, woe to you! You perished either by pride or by neglect and laziness.

As long as you have not yet entered the valley of tears, your inward man serves the world. This means you still lead a worldly life and work for God only outwardly; your inner man remains sterile because his fruitfulness begins with tears. When you do reach the valley of tears, you will know that your mind has left the prison of this world and has entered upon the path of a new time and has begun to smell the perfume of the wonderful new air. The tears begin to flow because the time of the birth of the spiritual child is near. Our common mother, Grace, wishes to produce in us in her own mysterious way the divine image so that we may see the light of the age to come. This phenomenon of tears is not the same as that which is experienced at times by solitaries, sometimes while they are contemplating, sometimes while reading or praying. I speak not of a passing experience but of tears that run unceasingly day and night, like a river, for two years or more. Perfect serenity of mind follows upon this. And with it, according to our measure, our mind enters into the state described by Saint Paul the Apostle. In that peace of mind, one begins to contemplate Divine Mysteries. Then the Holy Spirit opens heaven to the contemplative. God comes to dwell in him and resurrects in him the fruit of the Spirit. But listen further: once you enter into the region of the purification of your thoughts you lose the abundance of tears and they come only in a proper time and measure.

I stopped and looked at Father Michael. "I see that you have wept a great deal in your life, Father Michael."

"Yes, I have," the Staretz answered simply.

"I do not know why, Father, but one book moves me much to tears whenever I read it, even when I am reading it in the British Museum in London."

"It is a good book, Brother Sergius?"

"Yes, it contains a boy's reminiscences of his childhood in a pious Moscow family in the last years of the reign of Alexander II."

"Yes, my friend, in our age of unbelief and carnal life we have become cold. Tears are considered a manifestation of pitiful weakness, something to be despised — good, perhaps, for old women, but no one else. On the other hand, a stony indifference and a hardness of heart are regarded as virility, self-possession, sangfroid. But, in truth, such an absence of tenderheartedness is merely a sign of spiritual death. A Byzantine mystic once said that those who go to Holy Communion without tears and a tender heart, and still more those who, celebrating the Holy Liturgy, remain stonily indifferent, all of them eat and drink the Body and the Blood of the Lord unworthily. They are subject to condemnation. Therefore, cultivate tears and tenderness of heart, because only through them can we come to the purification of our thoughts. There is no other way."

"Tell me, Father Michael," I continued, "what can you say of the Light of Tabor? I have read several descriptions of that Light. For instance, in the fifth volume of *Dobrotolubiye* (the Russian version of the *Philokalia*) there is a description of that Light as seen by Saint Symeon the New Theologian. The experience is described in the third person, of course, according to the custom of the times. I copied the description, and here it is: 'Once, when he stood up in prayer, saying more with his mind than with his lips: "God, have mercy on me, a sinner," he was suddenly illuminated from above with the resplendent Divine Light, which filled the room. At that moment the young man forgot that he was in the room and under the roof. He was surrounded by the Light on every side and he did not know whether he was still on earth or not. The young man then lost all earthly cares and anxieties. Nothing earthly or carnal came to his mind. He was all melted into this immaterial Light. It appeared to him that he himself became light. He forgot all that went on and was filled with an indescribable joy. Afterward his mind ascended to heaven and he contemplated there another Light, much brighter than that around him. And he saw in that shining Light the Staretz who gave him the rule of prayer and the treatise of Saint Mark the Ascetic.' "

"In the life of Saint Symeon," Father Michael answered, "this vision appeared in the very beginning of his conversion. The Light of Tabor is the grace of God, given to those whom he wills. So it is also with the tears of grace. They are unobtainable by any effort of ours. The vision of Divine Light filled Symeon with tears. The Lord gives this Light as sign and promise, either to urge a man to go the right way or to retain him in it."

"I read of similar visions," I continued, "in the life of Saint Tikhon of Sadonsk, Abbot Anthony Putilov of Maloyaroslavetz, and the Megaloschemos Ignaty, restorer of Zadne-Nikiforovsky Pustuin, in the province of Olonets, who died in 1849 at the age of seventy. Father Ignaty writes: 'Once, when I was sitting in my cell meditating and tears were streaming from my eyes, I fell into something like an ecstasy. My soul contemplated the immaterial Light and I saw myself as made of light and my body dead, abandoned by the soul.' Dr. Rozov told me of a similar experience he had when, in 1926 in Pskovo-Petchersky Monastery, I discussed various spiritual phenomena with him."

"If you have experienced something similar, or do sometime in the future, meditate much on the conversation between Saint Seraphim of Sarov and Motovilov. This conversation, described by Motovilov, was published by Nilus shortly before the First World War. I have the first edition of this remarkable Motovilov manuscript. Here it is. Take it and read aloud the marked passages and I will comment on them." I took the booklet from Father Michael.

I began reading the words of Saint Seraphim to Motovilov:

"Prayer, fasting, vigils, and all other Christian deeds however good they may be in themselves, are, nevertheless, not the purpose of Christian life, although they are needed to attain it. The true purpose of Christian life consists in acquiring the Holy Spirit of God. Note, Father, that only deeds performed for Christ's sake bring us the fruits of the Holy Spirit. Anything that is not performed for Christ's sake, however good in itself, does not bring us a reward in the future life. For this reason the Lord Jesus Christ said: 'Everyone who does not gather with me, scatters.' The acquisition of this Spirit of God is the true goal of our Christian life, while prayer, fasting, alms, and all the other virtues for Christ's sake are merely means toward the first. . . . Indeed, every good work for Christ's sake earns for us the grace of the Holy Ghost, but prayer gives the most, because it is always at our disposal as a means to acquire the grace of the Spirit.

"With all other virtues for Christ's sake it is not the same. Either we lack the strength of character, for instance to presevere virginity, or we have no opportunity, as with almsgiving. It is different with prayer. Everyone may use it everywhere — wealthy and poor, nobleman and commoner, strong and weak, healthy and sick, just and sinner. Great is the power of prayer, and it is suitable for everyone. By prayer we are honored to talk with our all-good God and Savior. Yet there is only so much we can do, till the Holy Spirit overshadows us, in the measure of his heavenly grace known to him alone. When by his good will he visits us, we must cease to pray. Why pray then: 'Come,' et cetera, when he has already come to us in order to save those who trust in him and invoke his holy Name?"

"Father Michael," I said, interrupting the reading, "this passage is not quite clear to me. Is it true that when the Holy Spirit descends upon us, our prayer stops?"

"Yes," he said, "that is true. All the mystics have taught this. Prayer exists whenever we make an effort to say it in whatever form, but when the Holy Spirit overshadows us, no effort is needed and our prayer ceases. When the Holy Spirit descends upon us, we remain continually in prayerful sentiments toward God without words and without images. This is unceasing prayer. Now continue your reading."

"If, for instance, Divine Grace grants you prayer and watchfulness over your thoughts, pray and watch. If Divine Grace gives you the ability to fast with profit, do so. If you are attracted to works of charity, this is your way. Judge likewise of every good deed done for Christ's sake."

"You see, Brother Sergius," Father Michael interjected, "everyone has his own vocation from the Lord. One is attracted to the solitary life, another to fasting, a third to almsgiving, a fourth to virginity, etc. Whatever approach brings you nearer to God, do. Father John of Kronstadt had one vocation, while Bishop Theophan the Recluse had another. The first was a preacher and the second a writer. The first was continually with people, while the second received no one. And yet both were holy men. Go by your own way without judging other people or which way is best. The Savior forbade his disciples to do this."

I continued reading:

> "We in our time, because of our general indifference to our holy faith in our Lord Jesus Christ and our lack of attention to his Divine Providence for us, have reached such a degree of indifference, we may say, that we have abandoned true Christian life altogether. We now consider strange the words of Sacred Scripture where the Holy Spirit says by Moses: 'And I then saw the Lord walking in paradise,' or when we read in the Epistle of Saint Paul the Apostle: 'We went to Achaia and the Spirit of God did not walk with us, and when we returned to Macedonia, the Spirit of God was with us.'

> "In many other places of Sacred Scripture we read of Divine Manifestations to men. 'Well,' some people say, 'those passages are hard to understand; how could those men see God?' And yet this is quite understandable. This misunderstanding came about because we gave up the simplicity of the original Christian vision, and under the pretext of higher education became so ignorant that we consider hardly possible things that the ancients understand clearly. The mention of God's Manifestation in ordinary conversation did not seem strange to them."

"All this is perfectly clear," Father Michael observed, "to anyone who leads a life of prayer. Divine Providence is always with us. If we labor for Christ, like the Apostle Paul, the Holy Spirit favors us, but if we fall into our own, agitated ways he leaves us. Generally speaking, works for God's sake progress easily, albeit with some obstacles in order to prove us. On the contrary, if obstacles grow all the time in spite of our best efforts, it is a sign that the Spirit of God is not with us and we should give up our undertaking. Read on, please."

> "Men saw God and the grace of his Holy Spirit neither in sleep nor in daydreaming, nor in disturbed, sickly imagination, but in truth, in reality. . . . When our Lord Jesus Christ had completed the work of salvation, after his Resurrection, he breathed upon the Apostles, renewing the breath of life lost by Adam, and gave us the same Adam's Grace of the All-Holy Spirit of God. On the day of Pente-

cost he sent the Holy Spirit to the Apostles in a mighty wind in the form of fiery tongues. This very firelike Grace of the Holy Spirit, given to us in the mystery of Holy Baptism, is sealed on the principal spots of our flesh as an eternal tabernacle of this Grace. The priest then says: 'The Seal of the Gift of the Holy Spirit. . . .' If we did not sin after our Baptism, we would remain forever holy and sinless, free from all impurity of the flesh and spirit, saints of God.

"The trouble is that as we advance in years, we do not advance in Grace and the Mind of God, as did our Lord Jesus Christ, but, on the contrary, by befouling ourselves, little by little we lose Divine Grace and become in various degrees sinful and even very sinful people. Still, if anyone, being awakened by Divine Wisdom, which seeks our salvation, decided for its sake to pray and watch over himself to attain eternal salvation, he must, obedient to its voice, repent truly of all his sins and acquire the virtues opposed to them, and thereby gain the Holy Spirit, who acts within us and builds there the Kingdom of God.

"The Grace of the Holy Spirit, given in Baptism in the Name of the Father and of the Son and of the Holy Spirit, in spite of the darkness surrounding our soul, nevertheless shines always with the light of the priceless merits of Christ. This light of Christ converts sinners to the way of penance, removing every trace of committed crimes, and clothes the former criminal once more with incorruptible clothing, the Grace of the Holy Spirit, to acquire which is the purpose of the Christian life, as I have already told you. . . .

"The Grace of the Holy Spirit is the light that illumines man. Many times, before many witnesses, the active Grace of the Holy Spirit has manifested itself around those people whom he illumined by his descent. Remember Moses after his colloquy with God on the mountain of Sinai. People could not look on his face, as he was shining with the unusual light surrounding him. For that reason he was obliged to appear before the people with his face veiled. Remember also the transfiguration of the Lord on Mount Tabor: 'And his clothes shone like snow, and his disciples prostrated in fear.' When Elias and Moses appeared, the cloud overshadowed the disciples, too, in order to hide from them the Light of Divine Grace. In this way the Grace of the All-Holy Spirit of God appears in indescribable light to all to whom God manifests it.

"Everything is simple to the wise man. Being in this mind, the Apostles always knew whether the Spirit of God was with them or not. Penetrated by him and seeing the presence within themselves of the Divine Spirit, they recognized that their labor was holy and well pleasing to God. They wrote in their Epistles: 'According to the Holy Spirit's decision and our own.' And only on that basis did they propose their Epistles as unchanging truth for the benefit of all believers."

"Now, my friend," said Father Michael, "read the description of the descent of the Holy Spirit witnessed by Motovilov. I will comment in due course." I resumed my reading with Saint Seraphim speaking to Motovilov:

" 'Why do you not look at me?'

"Motovilov answered: 'I cannot look at you, Father, because lightning streams from your eyes, and my eyes ache.'

"Father Seraphim said: 'Do not be afraid, lover of God, because you are now as shining as myself. You are now in the fullness of the Spirit of God, because otherwise you could not see me in that state!' And inclining his head he said, whispering into my ear: 'Thanks be to God for his indescribable mercy to you. You see, I did not even cross myself but merely prayed to God mentally in my heart and said, "Lord, make him worthy to see clearly with his bodily eyes the descent of your Holy Spirit, as you do when you manifest yourself in the light of your magnificent glory." And you see, the Lord accomplished at once the humble request of his unworthy Seraphim. Now we should thank him for this indescribable gift to both of us. The Lord rarely manifests himself in this way even to great ascetics. May this Divine Grace console your distressed heart as a loving mother does her children, on the request of the Mother of God herself. Why do you still not look into my eyes? Look simply and do not fear. The Lord is with us.'

"After these words I looked at his face, and an even greater and more respectful fear seized me. Picture to yourself the face of the man who speaks to you in the middle of the sun at its noonday brightness. You see the movements of his lips and the changing expressions of his face. You hear his voice and you feel that he keeps his hands on your shoulders, but you see neither his hands nor yourself nor him, but only the blinding light extending many yards in every direction, illuminating with a brilliant glow the snowy mantle of the meadow and the snow falling from above on myself and the great Staretz. Is it possible to picture my state then?

" 'How do you feel now?' the Staretz asked me.

" 'Exceptionally well,' I replied.

" 'But how well? What particularly?'

" 'I feel an inexpressible stillness and peace in my soul.'

" 'This, lover of God,' said Father Seraphim, 'is that peace of which the Lord said to his disciples: "I give you my peace; not as the world gives do I give you. If you were of the world, the world would love its own. But because I chose you from the world, it hates you. But be of good cheer, because I have overcome the world." To people hated by the world but chosen by the Lord he gives that peace which you now feel within you — "Peace," according to the word of the Apostle, "transcending all reason." ' "

"Do you see," Father Michael intervened, "the Light seen by Motovilov, Symeon the New Theologian, Schimonk Germanus, Saint Tikhon of Zadosk, and others is the same as that which the Apostles contemplated when the Lord underwent transfiguration on Mount Tabor, in order for them to see even in their lifetime that Kingdom of God come in power? Observe, too, that the Lord did not take all the Apostles up the mount, but only three of them. And yet all of these three abandoned him, and the Apostle Peter thrice denied him. Saint Symeon the New Theologian saw this Light when he was still a young man, and soon afterward returned to a worldly life. Motovilov was the pious owner of a country estate, and that was all. Yet he contemplated the Light of Tabor. The grace to see this Light is given only to those to whom it is needful, either to console them, as in the case of Motovilov, or to strengthen them, as with the Apostles. Read on, dear Sergius."

" 'What do you feel more?' "

I continued my reading of the notes of Motovilov.

" 'The exceptional joy of my heart.'

"And Father Seraphim continued: 'When the Spirit of God descends on a man and overshadows him with his Grace, the soul of the man overflows with an inexplicable joy, because the Holy Spirit makes everything joyful when he touches it. It is the same joy about which the Lord speaks in the Gospel: "A woman, while she is in travail, endures sorrow because her hour has come, but when she has delivered her child, she forgets her sorrow for joy because a man has been born into the world. In the world you will be sorrowful, but when I shall visit you, you will be joyful and no one can take away your joy." However, the joy felt by you now is consoling to your heart. It is nothing compared with that joy of which the Lord himself spoke through his Apostle: "Neither eye has seen nor ear heard, nor the heart conceived the well-being which God has prepared for those who love him."

" 'If the beginnings of this joy which are given to us now make us so well and gay in our souls, what shall we say of that joy which is prepared in heaven for those who weep here on earth? You, little Father, wept enough in your lifetime, and see with what joy the Lord consoled you even in this earthly life.

" 'What more do you feel, lover of God?'

"I answered: 'An extraordinary warmth.'

" 'What kind of warmth, little Father? We are sitting in the forest. It is winter, there is snow above us and beneath us. . . . What warmth could there be in such conditions?'

"I answered: 'Such warmth as there is in the Russian bath when water is poured on the heated stones and the steam rises in a column.'

" 'And is the smell the same as in the bath?' he asked me.

" 'No,' I replied, 'there is no such perfume on earth. When my mother was still living I greatly loved to dance, and used to go to dances and balls in the evening. My mother used to sprinkle me with perfumes which she purchased in the best and most fashionable shops in Kazan, but those perfumes were never as pleasing as these.'

"Father Seraphim, smiling pleasantly, said to me, 'I know that as well as you do, but I asked you for a purpose whether you felt this way. It is perfectly true, lover of God, no pleasant earthly perfume can be compared with that which we sense now because we are surrounded with the perfume of the Holy Spirit of God. You said that around us it is as warm as in the Russian bath, but look — neither on me nor on you does the snow melt, nor above us either. It means that this warmth is not in the atmosphere but within ourselves. It is the same warmth for which the Holy Spirit makes us cry out in the words of the prayer: "Warm me with the heat of the Holy Spirit." Because of this, hermits — men and women — did not fear the winter's cold, being clothed, as in warmest furs, in the vestments of grace made by the Holy Spirit. This must be so, because the Grace of God must dwell within us, in our heart.

" 'The Lord said, "the Kingdom of God is within you." By this Kingdom of God the Lord means the Grace of the Holy Spirit. Well, this same Kingdom of God is now within us while the Grace of the Holy Spirit shines and warms us, filling the air around us with various perfumes, and sweetens our organs of sensation with heavenly pleasure and our hearts with indescribable joy. Our present state is the same as that about which the Apostle says: "The Kingdom of God is neither food nor drink, but truth and peace in the Holy Spirit." Our holy faith does not consist of persuasive words of human wisdom, but in the manifestation of spirit and strength. We are now in that very state of which the Lord said: "There are some among those present who will see the Kingdom of God come in strength before they taste death." Well, little Father, lover of God, you understand with what indescribable joy the Lord God has rewarded us. This is what it means to be in the fullness of the Holy Spirit, of which Saint Macarios of Egypt says, "I was myself in the fullness of the Holy Spirit." Now the Lord filled my unworthiness with the fullness of the Holy Spirit.' "

I stopped reading. Father Michael sat in his chair, meditatively, with his prayer cord in his hand. "Did you understand, dear Sergius, the significance of this speech?"

"Yes, I understand now that the Light of Tabor is the shining of the Holy Spirit when he descends upon men; it bespeaks the fullness of the Holy Spirit."

"Good. Now continue reading the marked passages."

" 'Little Father, you are a layman and I am a monk, but it is of no importance. God sees true faith in himself and in his only-begotten Son. For that he gives richly from above the Grace of the Holy Spirit. The Lord is searching for the heart that is filled with love for God and for neighbor. This is the throne upon which he loves to sit in the fullness of his heavenly glory. The Lord listens equally to a monk and to a layman, a simple Christian, if they are both orthodox and love God from the depth of their soul. If they have faith in him, even as small as a mustard seed, they will both move mountains.

" 'The Lord himself says that everything is possible to him who believes, while Saint Paul the Apostle says: "I can do all things in Christ, who strengthens me. . . ." Therefore have no doubt that the Lord God will answer your request if it is made for the glory of God and for the edification of your neighbors. And even if your request is for your own needs or benefit, if they are necessary to you the Lord God will grant you all you ask for, because the Lord loves those who love him and will hear them and grant their requests.' "

"You see, dear Sergius," Father Michael observed, "how needful faith is. Without it, according to the Apostle, we cannot please God, because we must believe that he exists and rewards those who love him. Otherwise prayer is impossible. Again, our faith must be strong, free of doubts, because men of double heart will not be accepted. You wanted to know what the Light of Tabor is? Well, Saint Seraphim explains the matter very clearly. There is nothing to add."

On August 16, the very day of my departure from Uusi Valamo, I attended the Liturgy celebrated by Father Michael in his hermitage and took Holy Communion from him. Father Michael said the Liturgy alone in his private chapel. After breakfast I took my leave of Father.

I met Father Michael once more, in Pskovo-Petchersky Monastery in July, 1960. Blessing me at that time, Father Michael said as his farewell: "Continue your efforts. Keep contact with Father Ilian on Mount Athos, and the Lord will be with you."

About two years later, Father Michael died. He was buried with great solemnity and now rests in the catacombs of the monastery.

Archimandrite Ilian

Hegumen of Aghios Panteleimonos

I met Father Ilian for the first time in the autumn of 1954, when I
visited Mount Athos after my stay in Konevitsa and Uusi Valamo, in
Finland. Father Ilian was then confessor of the monks of the Holy
Monastery of Saint Panteleimon. During my first stay, I met him only
rarely and we had little opportunity to talk together.

When I visited Mount Athos once more, in the spring of 1957,
Father Ilian was presiding over the monastery on behalf of the sick
Hegumen, Archimandrite Justin. During that stay, I met Father Ilian
nearly every day and had many talks with him. He used to come to the
big, bright room that had been given to me in the old guesthouse above
the gate of the monastery. Most of this building was to burn down in
1968. In the course of its history, it had sheltered many distinguished
pilgrims, including members of the Russian Imperial Family.

Fine engravings of St. Petersburg, as well as portraits of Emperor
Alexander III and of his wife, Empress Mary, and of the Metropolitan
of Moscow, Philaret Drogoov, decorated the walls of my room. Two
large windows looked out into the court of the monastery. The doors
of my room opened onto a long veranda, where the blue wisteria was in
full bloom. From the veranda one could see the sea, far below. It was
April, the end of Easter week. The pure, warm air was filled with the
perfume of the blooming flowers. The April morning was sunny, gay,
and peaceful.

There was a knock at the door. Father Ilian entered my cell
carrying with him a stack of books from the library for me to read.

"I have been reading, Father Ilian," I said, "the story of the journeys, across Russia, Moldavia, Turkey, and the Holy Land, of Father Parfeny, a monk of Mount Athos. Do you know this book?"

"Yes, of course. I read it. That Father Parfeny, an Old Ritualist, was professed here, and he was a friend and spiritual brother to our celebrated confessor of those days, Hieroschimonk Jerome Solomentser. Father Parfeny's Staretz, Father Argeny, sent him later to Siberia. Father Parfeny became Hegumen of the Monastery of Guglitsi, near Moscow, and visited the Holy Mountain once more before his death."

"I copied some things for myself from that book, Father Ilian, because I find them very wise. Listen, for instance, to this instruction of the Schimonk John, a hermit of Vorona, in Romania, to Father Parfeny:

> "When you reach the Holy Mountain, choose for yourself an experienced Staretz, Father and Instructor. Commit to him your body and soul and be obedient to him unto death. Live where he sends you to live. The Athonite Startzy are superior to the Moldavian. I would like myself to live with them and to learn all that is needful. Indeed, I went twice to the Holy Mountain, but the Will of God and troubled times disallowed me to remain there for good and I returned to my Moldavian monastery.

> "Concerning the future beatitude and how it could be attained, I shall tell you briefly. Wherever you will live, wherever you will wander, everywhere and in each place, the power of the Lord and his mercy are present. You should live, of course, according to his will. No place sanctifies the man but the man sanctifies the place.

> "The will of God consists of the three principal virtues: faith, love, and hope. Faith comes first. It is the beginning of all the virtues. Without faith all good works are dead. The just man lives by faith. This faith is carried by fasting and is strengthened by prayer. Faith is perfected by obedience and the destruction of our self-will. In this way, it is acquired and grows up. If you are unable to acquire such faith, you cannot acquire either trust in God or love for God and neighbor. If you fail to acquire them and are unable to purify the inner man, you cannot overcome passions.

"Wherever you will live — do not put your hope on any mortal, neither the Emperor nor the Prince, neither in the Patriarch nor the Bishop, not in merchants nor in any man, because every man is a liar. Do not trust in wealth, in the glory of this world, in your rank. Wealth is like a morning dew. . . . Trust God alone. We must love the Lord God in such a way that we prefer nothing to him, especially not ourselves. The love of God is proved by our love of neighbor. Our salvation consists in the sacrifice of ourselves and in watching over our hearts and in the unceasing prayer of Jesus."

"Father Parfeny is right," observed Father Ilian. "People used to come to the Holy Mountain in search of spiritual direction. Once a Staretz is found, he should be obeyed. Wherever he sends his disciple, the disciple must go. We must live in accord with the Divine Will, that is, according to the commandments of Sacred Scripture, Church regulations, and the instruction of the Staretz. We must not rely on men, even the very best and just. Man is a flower. He blooms today, and tomorrow he is no more. Father John, Hegumen of Petchenga, was right when he told you that once you have acquired spiritual wisdom you should be Staretz to yourself, because Startzy are mortal, like everyone else. This was true of Father Parfeny. He was the disciple of a very great Staretz, Hieroschimonk Argeny, who guided the Russian monks on the Holy Mountain at that time. But once Father Argeny died, Father Parfeny became his own Staretz."

"Do you know, Father Ilian, that while in Uusi Valamo, I used often to discuss with Father John the teaching of the Startzy of Valaam on the Prayer of Jesus, and with Father Michael on it fruits? But Father Parfeny describes very well the institution of Staretz itself. He came to Staretz Argeny and told him that he was choosing him to be his Staretz and would obey his direction as to where to live and what to do. Father Argeny answered Father Parfeny in this way:

"You propose to make a great promise. If you persevere in it to the end, you will do well. Only, you must prepare yourself diligently to practice patience and to bear many sorrows and temptations. I will direct you not according to your taste or your desire, neither according to my own human inclination, but according to the will of God. The Lord God does not want that we, his servants, live in bodily comfort, carnal pleasures, and material well-being. He leads his faithful servants by a hard, narrow, and sorrowful road. You see now, my dear Brother, what is the way of Christ. To this world, the way of Christ is very sorrowful indeed. But if it is hard, it nonetheless leads to eternal beatitude, while the broad and comfortable way leads to perdition. I will lead you by the narrow and hard way, according to the will of God, although this way may appear to you cruel and unsupportable. Will you go by this way to the end? It is easy to begin, but the reward is given only to those who go on to the end. You came to the Holy Mountain with the intention to remain here for life, but it might happen that it will be necessary to send you away to a place of which you have heard nothing. Such a mission might appear to you intolerable and you might refuse it. Therefore, do not promise to obey me but look first for some other Staretz and confessor. There are many Startzy on the Holy Mountain besides me. They live well and achieve their salvation.

"And it is true, Father Ilian. When Father Parfeny was professed and started to live on Mount Athos as a hermit, his heart was content. But Staretz Argeny ordered him to leave for Siberia, to a town entirely unknown to him. After some resistance Parfeny submitted to his Staretz's order. He suffered much in Siberia before Metropolitan Philaret of Moscow, whose portrait is here, took an interest in him and changed his lot. In the end Father Parfeny became the founder and first Hegumen of Guglitzi. What do you say of all this, Father Ilian?"

"I will tell you one thing only, my friend: the ways of Divine Providence are incomprehensible for us. Very often, things that appear to us desirable and useful are not so in fact, while things we detest are really needful for our salvation. Father Parfeny was a pilgrim for many years, and he hoped to live quietly on the Holy Mountain and be consoled for his sorrows. In fact, he looked for some kind of rest and comfort. Well, Father Argeny saw through him and sent him to Siberia to worse trials, until Parfeny realized his state and surrendered himself entirely to the Will of God. It is a fact that we serve very often our own desires and comfort while we imagine ourselves leading a holy life and going by the right way. While we are in reality advancing fast on the road of perdition, we believe ourselves to be all right. No one is a good judge in his own case. This is why a Staretz is so useful.

"We need to be patient, in no wise precipitous. If our business is from God it will right itself in the end, but if it is merely our own illusion all our efforts will come to nought. Surrender to the Lord your way and he will perfect it. We need great spiritual experience to be able to select a correct way, especially in very complicated situations. As you know, I am a native of the province of Yaroslav, from Rostav. My childhood and early youth I spent in St. Petersburg. I visited Valaam, but I did not enter that community, but entered the Desert of Glinsky, where I spent three years. But I did not remain there to make profession. I came here to Aghios Panteleimonos, and here I have stayed. In 1932 I was sent to Siberia, but I did not remain there, as Archimandrite Parfeny did, even though it has often been sorrowful for me for many reasons.

"Remember always: if your way of life is hard and sorrowful, it is correct; but if you live in comfort, wealth, and honor, and still more, in carnal pleasures, you are on the road to perdition. It is quite impossible to attain serenity of mind without enduring many sorrows and for many years. We dislike sorrows, although they benefit us. And we are attracted fiercely to the comfort and pleasures that destroy us spiritually and bodily."

"I also love very much the following passage from the counsel of Father John of Vorona to Parfeny:

> "When I came to the Monastery of Neamtu and heard from Father Paisios how to begin and how to continue the Prayer of Jesus, I started to practice it. This Prayer appeared to me so sweet that I preferred it to everything else. For that reason I avoided other monks, loved silence, used often to retire to solitude, ran away from all temptations and, most of all, idle talk. For the sake of the Prayer, I traveled twice to the Holy Mountain, fatigued myself with obedience and hard labor, metanias, and all-night vigils, in order to attain to unceasing prayer. For the sake of the Prayer, I often used to stay in solitude. In order to obtain it, I used up all my strength and became very weak. I continued in this way for many years and gradually the Prayer began to deepen. Afterward, when I lived in the Skete of Pokrov, the Lord visited me because of the prayer of Father Platon.

"Indescribable joy overshadowed my heart, and the Prayer started to run by itself. It is so sweet now that it does not allow me to sleep. I sleep only one hour in twenty-four and that sitting up. And I rise up again as if I never slept. For even while I sleep my heart watches.

"And the Prayer started to produce its fruits. It is true, the Kingdom of God is within us. There was born within me a love for everybody — something indescribable — and tears. I want to weep unceasingly. The Scripture of God, particularly the Gospels and the Psalms, became to me so sweet that I cannot enjoy them enough. Every word astonishes me and makes me cry much. O God, you manifested to me your unknowable and mysterious wisdom.

"Often in the evening, I rise up to read the Psalms or enter into the Prayer of Jesus, and I experience ecstasy. I go out of myself, whether in the body or out of the body, and whither to I know not. God knows. When I come to myself, the sun is rising. But temptations of the flesh beseige me to torment me in order to keep me humble. I cannot live with people, especially with lay folk; I cannot even talk to women. More than forty years passed in Moldavia without a woman visiting me, although many wanted to talk to me. I always refused to see them, saying I was ill. I experienced many temptations and sorrows from our foe, the devil, who still torments me."

"Well, dear Brother Sergius, one must spend many years in trials before reaching the state of John of Vorona. We must progress slowly, step by step. Those who want to reach the goal all at once are easily captured by the enemy and fall into spiritual delusion.

"Believe me, my friend, we need most and always humility. Without the latter, disputations and dissensions are unavoidable. Everyone wants to maintain his own point of view and impose it on all others. In this way, the disputants go continually and imperceptibly farther and farther from truth, incited by the devil. The Startzy of Optino advised all to use the Prayer of Jesus vocally as a means to attain to repentance, while the Prayer of the Heart they advised to be used rarely and only by those who overcame their passions and were under the guidance of an experienced Staretz. The wise monks of Optino thought that it was too daring to practice the Prayer of the Heart before conquering passions. Such boldness can easily lead toward an incurable delusion. Be always humble, my friend, and you will never be ashamed."

A few days later, Father Ilian again visited me. "I found in your library," I told him, "two manuscripts that interested me very much. The first is, most probably, the original of the well-known *Tales of a Russian Pilgrim*, and the second is *Notes of the Nun Panteleimona*."

"Yes, our Russian manuscripts are still unsorted and I believe some good finds can still be made. We have no one to undertake the work of cataloguing them. The number of our monks decreases continually. They are not numerous enough even for the essential work."

"I read several times, Father Ilian, the *Tales of the Pilgrim*. What do you think of them?"

"I think as Staretz Ambrose of Optino did when he wrote to a nun: there is nothing contrary to faith in the *Tales of a Pilgrim*. The latter lived free, unbound by cares and duties. He practiced prayer in the way he wanted. For monks living in community and especially for those with responsibilities, his way of life is not possible. Cenobites, since they are bound by various duties, can practice the Prayer only when they are free; the rest will be completed by obedience."

"I believe, Father Ilian, that only hermits or pilgrims can really practice the unceasing Prayer of Jesus. Staretz Michael told me the same in Uusi Valamo. Here, on Athos, the unceasing Prayer of Jesus is practiced mostly by the hermits of Karoulia.*

"Tell me, Father: Why are nearly all your conventual offices performed at night?"

"Such is the ancient tradition. Saint Isaac the Syrian wrote: 'Every prayer that we say at night is more important than all our work during the day.' The sweet feeling so well known to the faster during daytime is a reflection of the light flowing from our nightly monastic labors. This is very important in order to pacify our continuous stream of thoughts, which can be vanquished only by repentance and unceasing prayer."

I had many talks with Father Ilian. Once, I asked him about the practice of the Prayer of Jesus in the world, whether this is good or not.

"It is good, my friend," Father Ilian answered. "Father John of Kronstadt was a parish priest, and thanks to the Prayer of Jesus reached great saintliness and became a noted miracle worker and healer. He wrote in his book *My Life in Christ* that it is far better to say five words from the heart than to recite a multitude of prayers without attention and tender feeling. He also writes that when we pray we must be full of attention in order that our inner man may pray with the outer. If not, the devil will occupy our attention during prayer with his distracting thoughts, especially blasphemous and impure ones. This happens to quite a few even in church and on festive occasions. We must not lose our courage and give up prayer, but persevere in it. In due course the devil will retreat."

"Tell me, Father Ilian, could a busy man pray quickly and yet purely?"

"Yes, he can. The same Father John affirmed that those who learned interior prayer might do so. For that, our heart must sincerely desire what we ask, feel the truth of the words pronounced, and be simple and pure. Such a prayer does not suffer from hurry. But to those who have attained the Prayer of the Heart, it is necessary to pray slowly, awaiting the response of the heart. Because, according to Father John, prayer is the elevation of mind and heart to God. It is clear that he who is attached to anything earthly, for instance to money, honors, and the like, or overcome by passions, like hatred or envy, cannot pray properly.

"And Father John also said very wisely: Remember always that the invisible is far more important in the world than the visible. It is when something unseen leaves the living creature that it loses its life and turns into dust. We all live by the invisible energy of God. Whatever man loves, whatever he turns to, this he finds. If he loves earthly things and they settle down in him, he will become earthly himself and will be bound up by those same things. On the other hand, if he will love heavenly things they will dwell in his heart and will make him fully alive. When man has God always in his mind, it means that the Kingdom of Heaven has come unto him. Thus this man sees God everywhere and realizes his omnipresence, goodness, and mercy."

Another day when I was discussing with Father Ilian the writings of Father John of Kronstadt, he said to me: "Why are we so unhappy and anxious when we do not receive something desired or lose some treasure? This is so because the wanted or lost thing was the idol of our heart and we abandoned the Lord, the Source of the living water that alone can quench our thirst. If we are really attached to God, neither our earthly losses nor an unfilled expectation in this life will sadden us. A fervent prayer accompanied with tears does not only cover our sins but also heals our illnesses and weaknesses. The ascetic is truly renewed as an eagle. When we are young and strong and inexperienced, we are tempted to think that Christ is far away in heaven and the devil is far from us. But, with age, we find that Christ and the devil are nearby to help us or to harm us. When we pray mechanically, without attention and devotion, it means that our heart is full of unbelief and indifference. Our heart does not realize then our sinfulness and our pride. Anyone can find out whether he is proud or not. The more ardent prayer is, the humbler the man; the more mechanical, the prouder."

I left the monastery one warm May day. Father Seriphim, the infirmarian, arranged a brotherly meal for, inviting Father Ilian. We discussed for the last time various spiritual problems and monastic needs. Both of my brother monks wished to accompany me to the little port of the monastery, where I boarded the boat to go to Tripiti. When the boat started to move out to the open sea, I looked back to the harbor, where these two monks were standing upon the sea wall.

I never saw Father Ilian again, but I corresponded with him continually. He died on January 18, 1971. His secretary, Father Abel, wrote his obituary, published in the *Journal of the Patriarchate of Moscow* in 1971. He was truly, as Father Abel wrote, "a son's loving Father. Always and everywhere he was an example to the Community. He used to come first to all the conventual services and to leave the Church the last of all. Even in the final days of his life, weighed down by illness, his strength visibly diminishing, he continued to attend all the Services. The faults of his brothers he used to cover up with his love, punishing none. In this way he used to correct everyone."

Father Ilian died in his eighty-eighth year and was buried in his monastery with all the rites observed on the Holy Mountain.

A Good Monk at Dionysiou

Father Euthemios

In 1954 I stayed for several weeks at Saint Panteleimon's, the Russian monastery on Mount Athos. It was an October filled with beautiful sunny days, warm and calm. One day, Father Ilian, the Spiritual Father of the community, suggested that I visit the Greek monastery of Dionysiou. He said they had a very fine library and, more important, there were some truly spiritual monks in the community. He especially urged me to speak with the Hegumen, Archimandrite Gabriel, and the librarian, Father Euthemios. The latter, according to Father Ilian, was what is called "a Fool for Christ," *yurodivini.* So one fine, sunny morning, I left Saint Panteleimon's for Dionysiou.

The little boat took me first to Daphni, the port of Mount Athos, and then on south. In Daphni I met two monks, hermits, from Karoulia: Father Nikon and Father Alexander. I had known Father Nikon since 1931, when we met in England. An officer in the Russian Imperial Guard and a brother of the Russian Imperial Minister in Belgrade, he became a monk on Mount Athos soon after the First World War. He traveled a good deal, collecting money for the small Russian monasteries, or kellions, on Mount Athos, which had suffered much since the collapse of the Empire and the advent of the Soviets because these small communities lived largely on the alms of the faithful. Father Nikon knew well how to describe his peregrinations in a picturesque and interesting way and was not slow to share his impressions. He well realized that much traveling and continuous contact with the world are not good for a monk, and so after a long and generous service, he retired to Karoulia, an area at the tip of the Athonite Peninsula, and lived there as a hermit.

Father Alexander was a simple, peasant monk. He had been in Russia at the beginning of the First World War and been prevented from returning to his beloved Holy Mountain for many years. He was now very happy to be back in the Monastic Republic.*

I had a prolonged talk with these two monks, both in Daphni and on the boat. They were en route to attend the patronal feast of Grigoriou. I told Father Nikon that I met two Athonite monks in the West. "Yes," he answered, "but that is not good." Father felt that a monk should not leave his monastery unless he is sent out by his superiors on lawful business, and then only for a limited time. It is not good for a monk to mix into politics, especially if that would prevent him from returning to his monastery. Neither is it good to leave the Holy Mountain, changing from one monastery to another in search of an easier life. Many monks leave the Mountain for this reason. They destroy the Monastic Republic.

Father Nikon had been an officer and knew well from experience that, once an officer begins to criticize the higher authorities and their commands, discipline is lost. Once an officer begins to be critical and unruly, the soldiers will be too. This was the situation on the eve of the revolution in Russia. A monk is a soldier of Christ, who must obey his superiors and live a frugal, humble, and self-effacing life. Comfortable, easy living was never good for monks. All history demonstrates this, and it is as true in the East as in the West. Once monks begin to be well off, they degenerate. Many Latin monasteries lead a very comfortable life, and that is dangerous. Many Russian monasteries in the Empire also lived far too well. And notice, the richer the monastery is, the fewer vocations it attracts, and they are not especially good ones.

It is true, of course, that external observances alone cannot save us, but slackness is equally bad. Penance, prayer, humility, and charity are necessary for salvation, but how can a well-fed, comfortably living man pray with the proper humility and a spirit of penance? Services and even private prayer will be monotonous for such a monk and cause ennui. He would prefer bold intellectual speculations in theology and long Services to exercise his love and knowledge of music or any distracting activity that will keep him occupied. Father Nikon felt that to pray well, to meditate fruitfully, one must live in Karoulia as a hermit in that dire poverty which generates humility and compassion. The wealthy man rarely has compassion — otherwise he would not be wealthy. He is usually indifferent to the suffering of others. It is for this reason Christ said that it is difficult for a rich man to enter the Kingdom of Heaven.

"Isn't that true, Father Alexander?" Father Nikon asked his silent companion.

"Yes, it is true. The poor and oppressed have far more compassion and love than those who are well off," Father Alexander answered. "I noticed this during my troubled years in the Soviet Union. The newly rich Communist officials were hard on people."

Our boat had moved southward. I looked back on the imposing mass of buildings that constituted Saint Panteleimon's; all was bathed in warm October sunshine. At the beginning of the century, the monastery was able to house at least three thousand people. There were about two hundred monks, novices, and postulants, and the vast guesthouses could accomodate a thousand pilgrims. The First World War and the Russian Revolution put a stop to the stream of postulants from Russia, while the Greek Government did not encourage Russian émigrés to enter Russian monasteries on Mount Athos. As a result, all the Russian houses started to decay; soon there were many old men and no young ones. In 1954 the community of Saint Panteleimon had only about seventy surviving monks.

Our small boat passed along the western coast of Mount Athos and approached Grigoriou, a picturesque monastery built on the very edge of the water on a slight prominence. There my Russian companions and other monks left the boat to attend the patronal feast. I continued on my journey with a couple of monks and two Greek police officers. The coast became more and more rugged. The steep slope of the mountain reached right down to the water's edge and the terrain became ever more wild. Here and there, one could see small hermitages set into the mountain.

"Look up," said one monk to me in Greek. "Simonos Petras."

I looked up. A white monastery with blue galleries, built boldly on a great rock, stood silhouetted against the dark blue sky, a hymn to God in stone. It looked to me like a Tibetan monastery. Simonos Petras certainly is not only pituresque, but impressive. The boat rounded a promontory and the monastery quickly disappeared from sight. Soon we were approaching another, a gray-white citadel set high above its port on a rocky prominence. It was Dionysiou.

At the port, I disembarked, as did also the two Greek police officers. We started to climb up to the monastery along a steep, rough road. The officers began speaking to me. They said that their head-quarters on Athos is in Karyes, the capital of the Monastic Republic, but they also have permanent police posts at Saint Panteleimon's, the Great Lavra, and Vatopedi. The other monasteries, they visit only from time to time. Their job is to control the movement of foreigners and to watch for smugglers of rare books and icons, many of which have been illegally removed from Athos to Greece and abroad. No book, manuscript, icon, or any ancient ecclesiastical object may be taken from Mount Athos without proper permission.

We approached the gate of the monastery. It was already beginning to grow dark, but the gates were still open. A young monk met us and led us to the guesthouse. We crossed the inner court and went up a narrow staircase to the dining room, where supper awaited us. The guestmaster, a Greek from Macedonia, spoke Bulgarian. Supper was lively, because the monks feted police officers well. During our meal, a tall, ascetical-looking monk entered the room and, after saluting the company, addressed us in excellent Russian. He was Father Euthemios.

Born in Asia Minor, Father Euthemios early went to the Caucasus, where he became a licensed accountant. He never married, and after the Bolsheviks rose to power, he left Russia and entered this monastery on Mount Athos. He could not return to his native Tre-bizond, for all the Greeks had been expelled from there by the Turks after the disastrous Greco-Turkish War of 1922. Dionysiou was founded by Greeks from Trebizond many centuries before, and na-tives of that city usually entered Dionysiou when they became monks on Mount Athos. Of the twenty sovereign monasteries on the Holy Mountain, seventeen are Greek, and each usually receives the natives from one well-defined region: Macedonia, Cyprus, Asia Minor, the

Islands, etc. At the time of my visit, Father Euthemios was librarian. He was not a priest. Priests are few in number in Athonite monasteries. Like the early monks, nearly all are laymen.

"Do not stay here and talk for a long time," Father Euthemios said, "otherwise you will be late for the Morning Service in the church."

After Father Euthemios had left, the officers looked at each other and asked the guestmaster, "Who is that impressive monk?"

"Our librarian," he answered. "He is a bit unusual, an eccentric, or as the saying has it, a 'Fool for Christ's sake.' "

It was late when I reached my room — a very large one, simply furnished. I stepped out on the balcony, which overlooked the sea far below. The night was still and warm, the air pure and richly scented. "What peace and beauty!" I thought as I returned to my room and retired.

Father Euthemios was right! I overslept and missed the Morning Service! After dressing in the candlelight, I went down to the church. Passing along several dark corridors and staircases, I entered. Orthros* had just ended. Some old monks dozed in the dark narthex, waiting to go back into the church for the Liturgy. The tall, dark figure of Father Euthemios appeared from nowhere. "I told you yesterday," he said to me quietly, "to go to bed early so you would not oversleep, as you have done — but never mind; come with me."

He then led me into the church. Only a few oil lamps flickered in the darkness. Father conducted me to the stall next to that of Father Superior and again disappeared into the darkness. The church had its own air of mystery. A few red lamps burned before the golden iconostasis and the icons on the stand. Hieratic saints solemnly looked down from the blue walls. It seemed as though they, too, had come to assist at the Liturgy, representing the church triumphant. Silence reigned, except for the voice of the monk reading the prayers of preparation. An old priest came to ask my name in order to be able to mention it in the Proskomidia.* "Sergius is a good name," he said as he withdrew.

A very impressive monk, with the face of an ascetic and meditative eyes, entered the Superior's stall. It was Father Gabriel, Hegumen of Dionysiou, one of the most revered figures in the Monastic Republic. The Liturgy began. It lasted several hours. The Byzantine chant was perfect in this old Athonite church. All notion of time and space vanished. It seemed as if time were no more — that we were in eternity with those saints on the walls, participating in the never-ending praise of God.

After Liturgy, Father Euthemios brought me to the Hegumen's reception room, and the usual refreshments were served. I told Father Gabriel about my latest journeys and my forthcoming visit to Patriarch Athenagoras, in Constantinople. I also shared with him my impressions of Mount Athos and especially of Saint Panteleimon's. The Hegumen told me it takes a few months at least, and a stay in several monasteries, to understand life on the Holy Mountain. He was glad that I had taken the first step. "Prayer," he said, "is the most important thing; all other things are secondary even though they be necessary or even unavoidable." He wished me a happy and profitable stay on Athos as I took my leave.

I had several talks with Father Euthemios during my stay in Dionysiou. I soon realized that he was indeed a "Fool for Christ's sake." He was very severe on himself and toward others. The slightest weakness brought a severe reproof. As I had already met some Fools for Christ's sake, I understood Father Euthemios' way of speaking.

"The thing we need most," he said, "is humility, and this cannot be acquired without much suffering. We love to be honored and made much of, and we hate to be humiliated. It is painful to teach people humility, especially those in high positions. And yet they have most need of such lessons. If men do not teach them, God will, by destroying them, as happened with Hitler, Mussolini, and many others. Even in the Church, even among bishops and abbots, there is far too much pomposity and intolerance. In Russia it disappeared, because the Bolsheviks taught such a lesson that it will take a long time for anyone to forget it. The Communists are the scourge of God, sent to teach us the path of virtue."

Father Euthemios went on to recount a story:

There was once a holy monk known for his prophecies, and there was a Bishop who wanted to be Primate. One day, the Bishop called on the holy monk. The latter, seeing him, took no notice of him, but continued his exercises, leaving the Bishop standing at the door of his cell. The Bishop, a proud man, became furious. "Is this the way you treat bishops, proud monk?" he asked.

"It is not good for a Bishop, my Lord," the monk answered, "to take a monk from his prayer in order to engage him in vain and foolish conversation. Be humble and keep still. If you do so, you might well receive the Primacy, but if you continue to act as you are now doing, trying to please people in high station, you will never attain the Primacy. Instead, you will lose your diocese and be sent to do penance in a strict monastery under a harsh abbot. Do you understand what I am saying? Now you may go."

The Bishop went to the Abbot and complained: "That monk is an uncouth and bold man. He offended me greatly. He should be punished."

"Well, my lord," the Abbot answered, "I told you that he is a Fool for Christ's sake, and says candidly what others hide in order to please people. I warned you not to consult him unless you wanted to be humiliated."

What the monk predicted actually happened. Instead of becoming Primate, the Bishop was deprived of his diocese and sent to do penance in a monastery. After some years the Bishop was freed and returned to consult the monk — this time very humbly.

"Well, my lord," the monk remarked, "you know now that pride and the favor of the great of this world lead to destruction. But as you have humbled yourself, you will be exalted, though not in the way you think. Retire to a monastery and there you will experience spiritual joys of the highest order, before which all earthly honors are nothing."

Father Euthemios assured me that he was rude to the Hegumen and others in order to keep them on the right road, and that he had spoken severely to me on my arrival for the same reason. He went on to say: "Remember always, my friend, that humiliations are good for us and praises are bad. I wouldn't advise you to be rude to others, as I so often am, because you have another vocation, but never try to please people by flattery. This is bad for them and for you."

I then questioned Father on my own behavior. Should one tell only the truth, neither minimizing it nor exaggerating? Such a course would not be easy, of course, but it seems to be the only way.

Father agreed, and went on: "All lie, some more, some less, some openly, some discreetly. Because we commit sins all the time, we must pray all the time. This is the reason for the Jesus Prayer. Remember also that the harder life is for you, the better. Nowadays everybody looks for comfort and easy living, but this is destructive to the soul and also to the body."

Such was the substance of my first long talk with this Fool for Christ.

"Avoid all daydreaming and vain speculation," Father Euthemios told me when for a second time we sat down for a discussion. "They do no good. The devil uses them to lead us into sin, suggesting that we do this and that, tempting us either to look for popularity and honors or to engage in worldly pursuits — money, comfort, and the like. The heart that is perfectly free from all such dreams is filled with divine and mysterious thoughts; they play in it, like fishes or dolphins in the deep sea."

This wise Fool went on to counsel, "One should not try to speculate on theological subjects before his heart is purified. Otherwise he may very well fall into error or become an apostate. The Fathers have truly said, "every saint is a theologian, and every theologian must be a saint." It is quite easy to speculate and produce elaborate and seemingly correct systems of thought; living a holy life is a much more difficult task. In Greece, many theologians are educated in Athens and in Thessaloniki. These men like to speculate, but only a very few of them are ordained; they are not able to face the trials and difficulties of the priestly life or live up to the demands of the priestly state. They prefer to be schoolteachers. That promises to be an easier life."

At this point in our conversation, I asked: "Father, how do we fight against the tempting thoughts that come to us?"

"That is a wise question," he replied. "The continuous use of the Prayer of Jesus and watchfulness are the answer. We must keep our heart pure and avoid judging others. We must not be afraid of tempting thoughts. They will disappear in due course if we persevere in prayer and watching. Experience teaches us that. A true monk is one who has none but God in his heart. The monk who has something besides God in his heart is no longer a monk but an idolater, serving all kinds of devils: vanity, pride, mammon, and so on. The interior man suffers much from external impressions and sensations. Nevertheless, prayer, humility, and watchfulness over our thoughts will in due time repel all untoward thoughts, and in the purified heart the Divine Light will begin to shine.

"And remember," Father added, "no one can approach God unless he leaves this world." He went on to explain what he meant by "this world" — that whole complexity of temptations and passions that beset one in ordinary human life. For a sensitive man, it is difficult to live in the world and to see constantly before him all kinds of sin and vice. The devil does his best to seduce people and draw them away from God, involving them in all kinds of preoccupations that leave no time to pray properly and meditate quietly. In the end, such unfortunate people come to the conclusion that prayer is of little value. Every good deed is for them a prayer, they maintain. One venerates God in serving one's neighbor. As a result, they begin to reduce their personal prayers and to neglect the Services in the church. Little by little they begin to have a distaste for prayer, and go to the Services merely by custom or necessity. In the end they become virtual apostates. The easiest way to give up our faith is to cease to pray. And those who cease to pray become, in truth, unbelievers, although they may occasionally drop into church.

"If such be the case," I concluded, "there are very few Christians in the world, because only a few pray to God regularly and receive the sacraments well prepared."

Father Euthemios agreed. Real Christians have always been rare, and nowadays still more so. But it is not our business to judge others. We must judge ourselves, because each one must answer for his own deeds and not for those of his neighbor.

My last discussion with Father Euthemios took place on the eve of my departure. We were sitting on the balcony of his cell, overlooking the sea, and as we talked, the sun turned to gold and then sank into the horizon.

"Tell me, Father," I asked, "how difficult is it to attain to pure prayer?"

"Yes," he said as he gravely nodded his head, "it is very difficult indeed to acquire pure prayer. It takes many years. Without much effort and many sorrows, pure prayer cannot be established in the heart. No prayer can be won by easy and comfortable living. True prayer is possible only to him who has purified his heart with tears and sorrows. He who is pure of heart sees God. The Sun of the Tabor Light shines within him. He sees then what Motovilov saw when he discussed this very thing with Saint Seraphim of Sarov."

"Is it exceptional to see such things, Father?" I asked.

He replied: "It is exceptional surely in the sense that there are only a few people who have such purity of heart as to see the true Light. We do not take much care to obtain purity of heart, because we prefer worldly things: power, wealth, popularity, and the like. But if we reflect a bit we still see that all those things are uncertain and passing. They merely involve us in all kinds of vain activities and finally destroy us before the appointed time."

"What is impure prayer?" I asked.

Father answered very gently: When alien thoughts and anxieties remain with us during our prayer, then our prayer is impure. We cannot attain pure prayer until we leave the world and its temptations behind. Only then can our mind dwell on holy things. While in the world, we cannot attain to pure prayer, but we can be gradually purified by sorrows. If we endure sorrows manfully and humbly, they might well lead us to the gift of tears, which will speedily wash away our imperfections. It is quite possible to be saved in the world, even for the rich and powerful, but it is very difficult, as Christ said when speaking about the rich. If you want to be saved, realize your own frailty and weakness. Then you will realize that God helps us all the time, and this will make your faith in Providence unshakable. "He who believes in divine Providence is alwasy gay, because God carries him in his arms, as it were," he concluded.

I plied the saintly monk with one more question: "Do you think, Father, that short prayers are better than lengthy ones?"

"Yes, I think so," he answered. "The publican, the whore, and the good thief obtained their forgiveness with a single short prayer. Use a short prayer, but repeat it often with compunction and feeling. That is enough. But we must pray till we obtain the gift of tears. Then we can expect nothing more, because God gives the gifts of contemplation only to those to whom he wishes. It is enough if we obtain certainty of heart that our sins are forgiven. This feeling, combined with a perfect faith in Divine Providence, will make our lives a paradise here on earth.

It is impossible to describe all this. It must be learned by personal experience."

"And can I hope to have such an experience, Father?"

"Why not? All things are possible to him who believes."

I left Dionysiou the next morning. It was sunny and warm. Sea and sky were a deep, deep blue. Father Euthemios accompanied me to the little port. The boat came in and I boarded it. Soon it began to move away from the shore. As I looked back, the tall figure of Father Euthemios stood still on the pier, his stern yet radiant face a benediction.

The boat moved along the Athonite coast. The lofty white walls of Simonos Petras appeared against the deep blue sky, all bathed in sunlight — something of a vision. We passed Grigoriou, then Daphni. In due course I arrived at Saint Panteleimon's. I told Father Ilian of my talks with Father Euthemios. Father Ilian listened attentively and then said simply: "He is a good monk."

I never saw Father Euthemios again. He died the next year, 1955. But I think I would agree with Archimandrite Ilian. The most suitable epitaph for this Fool for Christ's sake would be: A Good Monk.

A Monk in Exile

Father Tikhon Voinov

My friendship with Father Tikhon extended over a period of seven years. I used to discuss many problems of spirituality with him either in Paris or in Villemoisson, where he lived in retirement. Father Tikhon was born in 1882. His Father was an officer in a Don Cossack regiment. His mother was a Pole. He received a very good education at home and in school and became an officer in the Staman Guard in St. Petersburg. He gave me very interesting accounts of life among the guards and at the Imperial Court at St. Petersburg in the beginning of the century. He graduated from the Academy of the General Staff, and in 1914 he was the youngest colonel in the Imperial Army, being only thirty-one years old. He survived the First World War as well as the Civil War, and in 1919 became an émigré, obliged to work for his living as a semiskilled laborer. As old age crept up on him, he was retired with a pension. He then entered a small Orthodox monastic community in Paris. During the time I was acquainted with Father, this community moved to Villemoisson, about eighteen miles from the French capital.

Father Tikohn had suffered much in his life, but this did not embitter him; rather, it transformed him into a loving old monk, much given to prayer and good works. There was something of Father Ilian in him, but there were also many differences. Father Tikhon habitually practiced the Prayer of Jesus and entered very deeply into it even though he did not have an experienced guide.

I first met Father Tikhon in March 1955, soon after my long journey to Konevitsa, Uusi Valamo, and Mount Athos. In 1957 I visited Mount Athos once again. In 1960 I visited the Soviet Union, the Lavra of the Holy Trinity in Zagorsk, and Pskovo-Petchersky Monastery. My acquaintance with Father Tikhon coincided then with the period when I was able to consult with Father Dorofey in Konevitsa, Father Luke and Father Michael in Uusi Valamo and Pskovo-Petchersky, and Father Ilian on Mount Athos. I discussed with Father Tikhon my impressions, what I saw, heard, and read. We used to converse almost exclusively on spiritual subjects. Father Tikhon usually avoided both small talk and reminiscences, but when he did engage in them they were, I must say, most interesting and colorful.

It was Father Tikhon's opinion that we neglect the "signs," that we do not meditate sufficiently on our past, out of which come our present and future. He thought, too, that we are neglectful in regard to meditating on our own names and the lives of the saints after whom we are named. Occasionally Father would write down his own meditations, which I found to be both deep and to the point. For him, nothing happened in the world without Divine Providence. Nothing in the world was purposeless or insignificant. Each person, thing, and event had their meanings. And all this was to be taken into consideration. In the world, Father Tikhon had been named Nicholas, which means, "victor," and his name in religion, Tikhon, means "happiness." He used to say: "I was a soldier but failed to realize the meaning of my name, to vanquish my passions and sins, and I was defeated in my life. Becoming a monk and receiving a new name, I found happiness."

Meditating on the apparition to Saint Mary Magdalene of the Savior after his Resurrection, Father Tikhon underlined the fact that she recognized the Lord only when she turned back, looked fixedly at him, and he called her by name: "Mary!" According to Father Tikhon, if we would truly meditate on our past, we could easily see Divine Providence guiding our lives and realize that Christ is always with us, till the end of the world.

As an infant, Father Tikhon had been baptized into the Orthodox Faith, but he lost it early and became an unbeliever. However, the atheistic explanation of the world and life did not satisfy him, so he searched first among the theosophists and the occultists and then among the extreme Protestant sects. In due course he returned to the Faith of his childhood. Later, a widower and retired, he became a monk. Still, some of the theological ideas of Father Tikhon were as daring as those of Teilhard de Chardin and often scandalized simple monks, but Father Tikhon never overstepped the boundaries of Orthodoxy, once he returned to Faith.

Father Tikhon was a humble monk, simple in his ways, and always ready to listen to and to help others. Many people came to him for advice. He was not unlike a true Staretz. I often shared with him extracts from the writings of Eastern Christian mystics. He fully accepted the view of Saint Isaac the Syrian that we cannot approach God in any other way than by unceasing prayer, which was for him as great a joy. Continuous visits by many people were for Father Tikhon a true cross, because they prevented him from speaking to God in unceasing prayer. While people usually came to him for advice or consolation, some abused Father Tikhon's kindness with idle talk or even condemnation of other people. The latter talk he usually stopped at once and was unwilling to receive again those who spoke in this way.

Father Tikhon was happy when I shared with him quotations from Saint Seraphim of Sarov. He especially liked these passages:

> Perfect love for God unites lovers with God and among themselves. Minds that have acquired spiritual love must never dwell on anything contrary to this love.
>
> Solitude, prayer, love, and abstinence are the four wheels of the vehicle that carries our spirit heavenward.
>
> Subdue the flesh with fasts and vigils and you will be able to reject the cunning suggestions of concupiscence.
>
> As it is God's business to rule over the world, so it is the soul's business to rule over the body.
>
> Concupiscence is destroyed by suffering and sorrow, either voluntarily undertaken or received from Providence.
>
> With what measure you master your body, with that same measure God will recompense you with the hoped-for good.

Father Tikhon usually interpreted this in this way: "We must rule over our body and never allow the latter to dominate us, because if we do we become a toy of all the passions and vices. I witnessed all that in my own experience and in the lives of others."

Other passages Father Tikhon especially liked are the following:

> If an ascetic desires the future as if it were already present, altogether forgetting everything earthly and more and more trying to experience the future life, this is a sign that he lives with true hope.

> Impassibility is good. God himself grants and strengthens this state in the souls of those who love him.

> Do not be lazy in active life and your mind will be enlightened.

> Solitude and prayer are the greatest means to acquire virtues. Purifying the mind, they make it able to see the unseen.

"Well, Brother Sergius," he once said to me, "you told me that Father Michael used to answer your questions before you asked them. He already knew what you would ask. Only hermits and recluses receive such a gift. For them it is not guesswork as with us sinners. It is clairvoyance. Life in Christ demands of us a continuous vigilance over ourselves, and this is attained only by unceasing prayer. I would like very much, my friend, to have a few talks with a Staretz, but they are very few now and I am old and an invalid."

One day, I encouraged Father Tikhon to say something about silence. He responded: "Truly, my dear friend, silence is a great virtue. There is an icon called 'The Angel of Holy Silence.' For a monk, especially an old one, the cell is like the Babylonian furnace burning up the old man of flesh. In the cell, by silence and by watching over our thoughts, we approach God, for it is said: 'Remain in your cell and it will teach you everything needful.' The cell makes an angel out of a man of flesh and blood. It introduces into us serenity of mind, which is nothing more than a foretaste of the Kingdom of God. I now understand so well what Staretz John of Vorona says: 'I can hardly be with people now, and especially with lay folk.' "

"Father Tikhon, with your love of prayer and solitude, is it hard for you to receive people who come to you for advice?"

"Yes, it is hard, but necessary. We must bear each other's

burdens. How can I expel these people? Especially here in Villemoisson, which is not a desert and people live around us. Often, talks are bad for me, because the devil pushes me into daring philosophical speculations and then forces me to defend my questionable thesis and so scandalize others. This is a serious sin. The Fathers used to say that every saint is a theologian and every theologian must first be a saint. We overlook this truth and enter into disputations before we have mastered our passions. The result is divisions, schisms, heresies, and apostasy. We should prove the truths of Faith by our humility and good living and not with cunning human speculations."

"What would you say, Father Tikhon, of the following saying of Saint Seraphim?

"If man does not worry too much about himself, for the love of God and for virtue, knowing that God takes care of him, such a hope is true and wise. But if a man trusts solely in his works, and prays to God only when sudden and unforeseen misfortunes overtake him, for he sees no means to save himself, then his hope is vain and false. True hope seeks only the kingdom of God and is sure that everything earthly that is necessary for this passing life will be indubitably granted. Our heart cannot be at rest until it has learned such a hope. The latter tranquilizes it completely."

"That is ccorrect, dear Brother. You and I know this from personal experience, and yet we fall frequently into vain thoughts, imagining that we can do something without God's assistance. In our contemporary world, God, we may say, is completely forgotten. If anyone turns to God in prayer, it is usually a sign that every human hope has been lost. Of course such a way of acting is vain and false. Generally speaking, we attain peace of mind only by passing through sorrows, because the route to God is through them. I know perfectly well that I would not have come to God or become a monk if I had not experienced many hard trials which lasted for many years.

"I consider the infallible sign of a spiritual man to be his dwelling within himself, his interiority; that is, keeping guard over thoughts and unceasing prayer. When a man attains to peace of mind he can, like Father Michael, radiate serenity on others. Once we attain peace of mind, we must keep it intact and never get excited when we are offended or humiliated. I am still unhappy when I am misundertood or blamed. And although I hardly ever judge other people, I occasionally tolerate idle talk, because I am still only a novice in true silence."

"What do you think of tears, Father Tikhon?"

"They are a great grace. There is nothing worse than stony indifference in prayer. Prayer without tears is cold, sad prayer. Tears melt away our insensibility and destroy our passions. Tears must not be despised. Among military people, brought up on stoicism, tears are considered to be shameful. Tears lead us to repentance and allow us to come through the most devilish temptations, preserving deep peace of soul, in which the devil cannot sow his seeds. When we maintain peace of mind, we can easily discover his insinuations. When our heart is in turmoil, the devil has full freedom. Therefore we must never undertake anything when our soul is sorely vexed and anxious. We must wait till our heart becomes quiet again, and then act."

In the spring of 1962 I had had a very strange dream, which I described to Father Tikhon.

"I think," the monk observed, "that this dream will come true. Yet as a rule we must not trust in dreams, forebodings, et cetera, but ignore them. It is so easy to err and become superstitious. Still, if dreams lead us toward a good deed, they might be taken for guidance. In such a case they may come from above, as we read in Scripture and in the lives of the saints. Because I was in intimate relationship with occultists for a number of years, I saw and heard a great deal. It is inadvisable and often dangerous to probe into the future, especially by our own will.

"We must preserve our purity of heart: 'Blessed are the pure of heart, for they shall see God.' Nor should we open our heart to many people, but only to our Spiritual Father. In the latter case our treasure remains safe from foes, visible and invisible. This discretion is especially necessary if we have passed through great spiritual experiences. I read of this in the Fathers and also have learned it by my own experience."

"Father, have you read the instruction of Saint Seraphim on how to distinguish between good and evil thoughts as they come to us? He says:

When a man receives something divine he rejoices in his heart but when he accepts something devilish he is troubled. The Christian heart receiving something divine does not demand confirmation from outside that the gift comes from the Lord, becaues the experience itself persuades the heart that the suggestion is from heaven. The heart feels within itself the fruits of the Spirit: love, joy, peace, long-suffering, goodness, charity, faith, meekness, and abstinence, as the Apostle Paul wrote to the Galatians. Whereas if the devil comes to us even in the form of an angel of light and suggests the apparently most innocent ideas, the heart nevertheless will experience some obscurity and confusion in its thoughts and turmoil in its feelings. Thus by the very different results produced in his heart a man may distinguish between the divine and the diabolical.

"Isn't this so, Father Tikhon?"

"This is perfectly true, my friend. When I associated with the occultists, I saw many astonishing things that seemed good, and yet I felt within my heart something disturbing, some confusion."

"The late Sergius Paulus, Father, who before his return to the Church consorted much with the sophists, said the same thing. I met his theosophical friends occasionally, and I must say that my impression was similar. I felt the same thing while reading Tibetan books. One feels that there is something hidden, unsaid, esoteric."

"It is well, Brother Sergius, that you were not attracted to those things, which have the power to captivate people. I believe it is far easier to convert to Christ a militant atheist, who is often really ignorant and a superficial thinker, than a theosophist, who is often the prisoner of some invisible power. The Tibetans do not deny the existence of such powers. They attribute things to the influence of the shamans. As far as we are concerned, we should not accept anyone but Christ. To play with spiritism of any kind is dangerous indeed. Anyone who denies that Christ is the Son of God and the only Savior is an antichrist, according to the Apostle. The Church teaches nothing different.

"We save ourselves by humility, unceasing prayer, and by love of God and our neighbor. We perish when we fall into daring speculations — as the Gnostics did — and neglect to lead a holy life."

Father Tikhon died in 1964. He was in search of God for many years, and finally he found him. He never seemed to reach the depth of Father Michael or the radiant joy of Father Ilian, but everyone has his own vocation. Perhaps this lack of depth was due to his theosophical connections. We hardly realize how much our past influences us and how difficult it is to discard the habits of thought followed for years. Still there is great merit in detaching oneself from a sinful past and returning to the house of God. This Father Tikhon did. And when he did, he strove with great humility to be wholly a man of God and a servant of man. And for this reason I have no doubts as to his great holiness and the wisdom of his teaching.

The Young Elder

Archimandrite Aimilianos

It had been a long, hot ride. Even after we left the sprawling, pastel suburbs of Athens and the rolling foothills ascending the rugged mountains, the crowded train had shown no sign of cooling. The vistas across the coastal plain were captivating: immense formal gardens with squares of wheat and olives marked off by stately rows of poplars. We arrived at Farsala over an hour late. There we changed to a small, narrow-gauge, one-car train that was to carry us west over the plain of Thessaly. We traveled for about an hour; then, suddenly, there leaped up before us and soared into the faultlessly blue sky a most incredible array of dark, weather-worn, granite monoliths. There is nothing in the West quite comparable to this unique geological configuration — a veritable forest of gigantic rocks of varied shapes. The nearest likeness would be the Montserrat, near Barcelona, but it has not quite the same awesome suddenness of immensity. Meteora is truly unique.

Clustered before the feet of this giant is the village of Kalambaka. It boasts a few second-class hotels, train and bus terminals, a rather prosaic village square, and a taxi service to ascend on high. One really gets one's money's worth on that taxi ride as the old Mercedes winds its way around and around and in between the huge, loftly columns of rugged stone.

Perched on the tops of these monoliths are some twenty-four monasteries. Most of them go back to the fourteenth century. Monasticism claimed these dizzy heights for herself four centuries after the first flowering on the Holy Mountain. The pioneers had to construct such scaffolds as had probably never before been seen, straight up perpendicular granite walls to frightening heights. And then all the makings of some rather large monastic establishments had to be hoisted up after them. As late as the 1920s, the only way to reach some of the monasteries was to be hoisted up in large rope nets. Even today, most of the supplies must be brought into the monasteries in this fashion.

Sad to say, most of the monasteries now stand empty. Six of them boast a few monks who courageously carry on, singing the offices, venerating the icons, preserving a precious heritage both spiritual and material, and offering as generous a hospitality as they can. The Greek Government has encouraged tourism and put in roads, bridges, and steps. And the curious come by the busload. This is why the one glorious exception in that holy colony has become like the other six. With the monasteries perched atop lofty spires, there is little room for a flourishing community to pursue a peaceful monastic life in the face of droves of visitors.

In September 1973 there was still one flourishing community. And that was the one I was on my way to visit: the Great Meteora, the Monastery of the Transfiguration. I had already heard about it in America from my Greek friends. At the Orthodox-Cistercian Symposium at Oxford University there was present a novice from this monastery who had come to England to study theology at King's College, London, and he invited me to visit his community. In fact he gently urged me. But the urging was hardly necessary: after what he told me of their Spiritual Father I began to look forward eagerly to the visit.

The old taxi came to a halt three hundred yards from the monastery. A deep ravine lay between the end of the road and the height on top of which the monastery stood. It was necessary to descend some distance on a steep winding path and then cross a narrow bridge. Here there is a loading station for the net that carries all supplies up into the monastic stronghold. Then we had to ascend through a tunnel cut in the granite and by steps set along its face. I was glad I had only a small shoulder bag. It was a hard climb — and for me a rather frightening one as my glance fell over the side of the steps to the floor of the ravine far, far below.

I arrived at the door at 4 p.m., just the time the monastery was reopened for afternoon visitors. That was good, for I do not know how one could have otherwise penetrated this monastic fortress. A letter of introduction to the Spiritual Father soon brought the handsome young guestmaster, Father Justin, to welcome me. We went to the recently renovated guesthouse. The quarters were very clean and neat, quite austere yet tasteful. There were but a few rooms for guests and a couple of small parlors. The second floor was occupied by the overflowing group of novices.

The customary refreshment was served: a tall glass of delicious cold water, so appreciated in this hot, dry land; a spoonful of candied fruit, and a demitasse of dark Turkish coffee. The ouzo was absent; this I would often find to be the case also on Mount Athos. Perhaps the great influx of visitors caused this, though I believe the reformed monasteries feel it is best to do without it.

I was soon settled in a modest cell with a breath-taking view out across the Meteora and down into the valley and the village of Kalambaka. Across one ravine, I could see the neighboring monastery, Valaam, where a small community guards a priceless inheritance of icons and manuscripts and welcomes an endless procession of tourists. Sounds carry and multiply around the granite towers, but for the most part the intense silence carried only the sound of the semantrons* and bells calling the respective communities to prayer. Father Serapion came with a hearty meal, which I had barely finished when Father Dionysios knocked on my door. What a joy it was to meet this radiant and intelligent young monk, who spoke beautiful English. Like most of the community, he had begun his novitiate while still at the university where he had first heard of the Spiritual Father.

Father Aimilianos, the Spiritual Father of the Great Meteora, was still a young man, not yet forty. He is not very tall, rather heavy-set, and his hair and beard are black and full. His face is lively, well rounded, with lines at the eyes, soft brown eyes, like the remains of Turkish coffee, and fairly bulging. There is almost always a smile playing about his lips. I found this to be true: there was always joy radiating from the Spiritual Fathers: Father Vasileios' face was constantly lighting up and giving birth to a warm, gentle laugh; Father Paisios was absolutely mirthful in a deep and intensely joyful way. On the other hand, most of the young monks seemed always to be deadly serious. Father Dionysios was an exception.

Father and I spoke together till the semantron summoned us to Apodeipnon.* I think our joy was equal in finding how much we were one in mind and spirit — how alike were our lives. He told me how Father Aimilianos had come to Meteora some ten years before, after having been very active in working with Christian youth. At that time, Meteora was like its neighbors, the refuge of a few old monks who were for the most part caretakers of a precious heritage. Happily, someone came to receive the inheritance. At first the Father lived a solitary life in a small hut that clung to the edge of the monolith, forty or fifty feet behind the monastery. After about three years, disciples began to come, and he was accepted as the Spiritual Father and Superior of the cenobium.* (This reminded me of the history of our Father, Saint Benedict.) When I visited, there were sixteen professed monks and ten novices under his paternal care. Most live at the Great Meteora, though some of the novices are still at the university. A part of the community goes periodically to one of the small, previously abandoned monasteries farther back in the Meteora, where they can find greater solitude and live more austerely.

Father Dionysios told me Vigils would be at midnight. In good Western style I rose at eleven-forty to be in good time. The semantron did not sound until 1:40 a.m. Midnight is the middle of the night, more or less. Only two monks came to the church for the Service, which lasted till 2:20 a.m. More than half the community were in deeper solitude at this time, and most of the others stayed in their cells to pray the Jesus Prayer. Father Dionysios explained to me that the three cardinal points of their life are the Liturgy* (in the renewed monasteries, it is celebrated daily), reading (primarily the Sacred Scriptures, but also the Monastic Fathers, the tradition), and the Jesus Prayer. Constant prayer is the ideal, and everything in the structure of the life is geared toward making it an actuality.

The semantron sounded again at three-thirty, this time a small one that was carried to all parts of the monastery. All who were present in the monastery came to Orthros and sang with vigor, using harmonies reminiscent of the Russians. I would find this again in other renewed monasteries, where a good bit of the solo singing of the

Greeks had been replaced by choral singing in the Slavonic tradition. The Service led right into the Liturgy, celebrated by the Father, the only priest in the community. All was beautifully done, with great dignity, in the half darkness of a few oil lamps. At the conclusion of the Liturgy I went forward to receive the antidoron* but was stopped on the way by Father Dionysios with gentle words. This degree of ecumenical sharing, now quite common with the Orthodox in the West, is not the practice in Greece. On my first day on Mount Athos a kindly Spiritual Father warned me of this.

At 8 a.m. the community gathered for "lunch." The fare was very simple and frugal — for the most part, what they themselves could provide: some stuffed peppers, homemade bread, goat cheese, grapes from their vines in the valley, and water from the fountain in the garden. After what for us in the West would be a long grace, a passage from Climacus was read on a sustained tone while we ate. The thanksgiving was longer than the grace.

As we came out from "lunch," tourists were already beginning to arrive. Cars and buses coming up the winding road make a lot of noise in this silent place. There are signs on the road asking visitors not to shout. Every sound re-echoes. The monastery is open to visitors from nine to one and from four to six.

Father Dionysios and I walked around the monastery and the top of the mountain. The views are breath-taking. This monastery, the first to be founded here, was established in the fifteenth century by Saint Athanasios. His royal disciple, Saint Joasaf, greatly enlarged the building. Their skulls are preserved in the narthex of the church. Except for the katholicon and the refectory (now serving as a museum), most of the old structures have been destroyed. The present guesthouse-novitiate was built in 1932. Some of the monks, like the Father, live in cells built into caves. Father Dionysios has a small house, seven by seven, on top of the mountain. His cell was truly a chapel, with many icons, lamps and candles, and a lectern. Besides these there were only a low stool and a very low wooden platform for sleeping.

Father showed me a fine anthology of monastic writings published in Athens in 1969 by Bishop Dionysios of Trikkala. (The Elder was to give me a copy of this before I left, and I have brought it home as a special treasure.) He spoke of the saints who lived on Meteora and of Saint Nectarios, whose picture had a special place among his icons. He is personally acquainted with a spiritual son of this saint. The saints are very much alive among our Orthodox brothers; indeed all tradition is. This is one area where they certainly can help us.

For Father Dionysios and his brothers, the three treasures of life are the Liturgy, Communion, and the Jesus Prayer. They sing the Liturgy with enthusiasm and joy. All are expected to be in church for Orthros, Liturgy, and Vespers. For the other hours they can pray in their cells. As I mentioned, they use some of the smaller monasteries farther back in the mountain for retreat — periods of fasting and intense use of the Jesus Prayer to obtain mystic prayer.

The Spiritual Father is called *Gerontas*, the "Old man" (even though he is young) or simply the Elder or "The Father." The other monks are called "Father," and the novices use their baptismal names. When they become monks, they will receive new names. Novices might be as young as fifteen — the Elder believes an early start is good for forming a true family spirit. Yet study and learning are appreciated in the preparation for monastic life. Most of the present monks were novices at the university. The novitiate usually lasts about three years, but there is no set rule. It can last much longer.

I had asked to see the Spiritual Father but had been told his schedule was full and there would be no time. After Father Dionysios and I spent the morning together, he served me the usual refreshments and went off to tell Father of our conversation. Before I finished the coffee, he was back to say the Father would see me for a few minutes. In fact we were to speak together for several hours, ending only when the last of the Vesper bells demanded we run for the church.

As our conversation opened, the Elder said quite simply, and in a way that was not the least bit offensive, that the East, Orthodoxy, had nothing to learn from the West. He then went on to inquire of my monastery and our Order. He expressed sincere joy about what he heard. He was especially interested in the system of general chapters and visitations the Cistercians use to try to maintain fervor and fidelity in their monasteries. He asked for a copy of their *Charter of Charity*. He had heard of the "Roman Synod" but was delighted when I related what Vatican II had taught about monastic and contemplative life. He asked me to send him these statements, so he could have them translated into Greek and shared in his country.

We went on to talk quite frankly about ecumenism. For Father, the division of the churches was of no concern, for the Church is one, transcending history, and ultimately will be in historical fact one. In the course of history the Church willingly cuts off parts to keep the essence dynamic, yet in its essence it ever remains whole and complete. As monks, we have four things to do:

1. agonize whether we are in the true Church — the spiritual one of union with Christ and the Father — for which Christ prayed;
2. know that it is by the power of God that we stand in the Church and pray;
3. pray without ceasing;
4. realize we are one with all in Christ's Body of all time and place.

We should be happy, because we are in the monastery and called to the "theoretical" life (we might say "the contemplative life," the life oriented to *theoria*) and not because many come to us. In our Western monasteries, where the ancient traditions are kept they have been westernized. We can best each keep the truth as we see it and stay where we see God wants us.

I expressed my joy that I was able to be one with them in offering the Liturgy that morning. Father's response was kind but firm. He appreciated my love, prayer, and piety and said he could not enter my heart to understand how I sensed myself offering the Liturgy with them. But for them I was a mere presence (which used not to be allowed — and still is not allowed in some monasteries on the Holy Mountain); only the Orthodox there present and throughout the world formed the worshiping community. This may sound like a hard saying. In theory the positions are rather rigid, but in practice a sincere Christian love prevails. At Vespers, Father himself came and incensed me. At Apodeipnon, Father Dionysios, who was presiding, asked the monk from Canada, the only non-Greek in the community, to recite the Creed in French — undoubtedly for my benefit. And the following morning, the Father sent one of the monks to invite me to enter the sanctuary to venerate the relics of my holy patron, Saint Basil, and many other saints.

Very sincerly, the Father expressed his regret that I could not stay longer. He said he would share with all the brothers the many things I had told him about monastic life in the West. The Father had to leave in the middle of the night to walk to the convent of the nuns, Saint Theodore's. This community had been started by the Father only a few years previous in response to the urgings of the sisters of some of his monks. The Mother (a sister of one of the monks) and two others are professed; all the rest of the twenty-three are novices; all are young and well educated. The Father walked there in the night three times a week to celebrate Orthros and Liturgy for them in their very small and crowded monastery.

During Orthros, Father Dionysios came to ask me if I would accompany him by taxi to Saint Theodore's, as the Father wanted to talk further with me and have me speak to the nuns before I left for Thessaloniki. I was delighted. A little incident occurred on our arrival that impressed itself on my mind and made me aware of a very important point. Father Dionysios had insisted on carrying my bag. I was a little embarrassed, but as he was a strong, young man and the host, I allowed it. When we arrived at Saint Theodore's, the Mother was out front (with a novice who spoke some English) to welcome me. Immediately, Father Dionysios let her take the bag. With two strong men there, to see this nun struggling up the stairs with my satchel did violence to my Western sensitivities. But my efforts to retrieve the bag only met with remonstrances. This is the way things are done in Greece. In the little details of life, how sensitive we have to be where another culture, another tradition, now stands. It is so easy to judge and evaluate all according to our own customs and present position.

When all the sisters had gathered, the Father and I carried on a dialogue that lasted over two hours. And the nuns asked their questions. They were interested in our monastic Order, the decisions of Vatican II on the contemplative life, our nuns, our Saints and holy

Fathers and Mothers of today. They asked that I send accounts of these to them. All too soon, it was time for me to get in the taxi again to continue on to Trikkala, Larissa, Thessaloniki, and the Holy Mountain. The Father and I exchanged the triple kiss of peace, and he gave me a small icon of my Blessed Patron painted by one of his monks. I think we all sincerely regretted the shortness of the visit.

The meeting of monks and nuns from the various Churches during the Orthodox-Cistercian Symposium was indeed a rich experience and opened hearts and doors. But I think I agree with what seemed to be the common consensus of our Orthodox brothers there. First, it would be better for us to meet in the monasteries, in our own natural — or supernatural — milieux. And, I believe, first we of the West must go to the East. It is easier for us, indeed it is immensely enriching for us, for we have come out of the East. Our brothers and sisters from Orthodoxy would find many more things among us difficult to understand and accept. First, they have to meet us in that context where they are at home and where we can so readily find ourselves at home. And in the sharing, if we are true monks and nuns, because of their true Christian spirit, they will quickly recognize us as true brothers and sisters. We must be sensitive to where they stand, and to the wounds. Tradition is so present and alive among our brothers and sisters — how we need to learn this from them — that the many offenses of the Middle Ages, the desecration of the Holy Patriarchal City, are not events of long ago, as we tend to perceive them. They are much closer and much more keenly felt. There are prejudices; I might say fragile prejudices, for they so quickly break down as it were and give way as Christian meets Christian in sincerity. So little is known about Western monasticism in the East (who of us thinks of translating into Greek, though we have done a lot of translating from Greek). As it gets better known and our brothers and sisters in Orthodoxy see how much alive is the common monastic tradition in many of our monasteries, then indeed monks and nuns will build bridges.

CONFERENCE OF ARCHIMANDRITE AIMILIANOS

On the Occasion of the Profession of Two Monks

Today, my dear children, we are dancing with joy around the holy altar. Today, again, the Holy Mount is celebrating. Who is so blind as not to see that at this hour heaven is brightly adorned, earth is rejoicing, the martyrs are leaping like surging waves, the saints are singing *Alleluia* to give vent to their desires and sentiments to God as you celebrate your mystical marriage.

You yourselves are leading this dance, for the day you have long awaited has come at last. The day that until now you have only envisioned in your dreams has dawned. The day your hearts have longed for has come at last: the day for you to be dedicated as unblemished lambs to Christ.

That most swift and skillful Hunter has captured your youthful hearts. He is dragging you behind his chariot, that he may bring you into his kingdom. On the one hand is he who has sought you day and night; on the other are you who would not close your eyelids until you were able to rest in Christ. You were both pursuing him as the hound pursues the hare. He has given himself to both of you, and now you are reciprocating by offering yourselves to him. You are dying to the world, to live only for God.

How can a worldly eye perceive what is not being brought to light? How can a worldly mind understand what is transpiring at this hour? But I see before me a miracle. You, Thenassi, my first child, from the time I met you, you have conducted yourself as being ever in the presence of God. You were still a young boy, still in short pants.

You could not even speak well. When you tried to say something, your cheeks quivered, your lips stammered, and your face flushed because of bashfulness. I observed you closely and secretly rejoiced, because I foresaw that one day I would offer you as a mystical victim, wounded by the darts of Christ; that, one day, before the whole Church, you would take an oath to live only for God. And now that time has come. Open your eyes and see. God himself is bending down to embrace you.

And you, dear George, my youngest child, but equally and even more beloved . . . when you were skipping and playing as a carefree child, God seized you. You heard his voice calling you, and as those who know you bear witness, quicker than the leap of a monkey, quicker than the wondrous decision of the sons of Zebedee, disregarding the voices of priests and great hierarchs, you asked to be allowed to put on the "robe of rejoicing," the mantle of the angelic state.

You became foolish in the eyes of the world but wise in Christ. My children, I feel like crying out, "Hide, you renowned of the earth! Disappear, you wise men of the world, lest these babes whom God has chosen put you to shame! Be still in your hide-outs and know the true God and see if anything exists that has greater glory or conceals more honorable wisdom than that which we have before us."

Truly, the poorest people are they who cannot understand what it means to offer oneself to Christ. Let them, therefore, live their prosaic lives and walk on the black asphalt. Let them be guided by traffic lights. They have never been able to see him who sends out the light and it goes forth, who makes the sun rise and bids the dawn to break, who lights up all the universe. Let them listen to the sound waves in the air — they can never hear him who calls out, "He who thirsts, let him come to me and drink."

Who can worthily tell of the beauty of this moment? When I find myself confronted with a tonsure,* my mind is in a whirl. It is not a human thing. Tonsure is as if the heavens rushed into space, as if eternity swallowed up time. Tonsure is a victory of the Church, a dissemination of the Holy Spirit, an abduction to divine life. In this hour of your tonsuring, divine grace and the human will are united. The angelic choirs begin the sacrifice, the heavens descend. Earth ascends, leading and offering before the altar of earth and beneath the altar of heaven, as gifts to God in this hour, your youthful lives, your two slain souls. For this is your intention: to slaughter yourselves for Christ.

But if we really ponder the matter, the objective truth is different. You do not offer yourselves as gifts to God — it is God who gives himself as a gift to both of you. In this hour you come to dwell with the saints; you stand on a level with the celestial powers although in the flesh, familiarizing yourselves with their state. You become beholders of God, bathed in the inaccessible and immaterial Light. Tell me, therefore, can anyone see anything greater than this on earth?

The most beautiful moments — truly and essentially unique — the most beautiful moments you can live are those hours when, keeping vigil during the night, you win God and place him under your command. These are the hours of ineffable sighs, when Christ visits you personally and changes your inmost thoughts. They are also the hours of painful and passionate seeking, when darkness becomes twilight and the twilight is swallowed up by the shining rays of the Trinity.

Yet these moments of human life that we are now living are more beautiful and emotion-laden and powerful. They have an eternal weight, these moments when you offer to the Bride, the Church, who flees to the desert to preserve her essence — when you offer "maniac lovers" to her. This is the hour when you throw at the feet of the Bridegroom of the Church souls intoxicated with his beauty, souls seeking the Invisible One with intellectual senses.

You have been snared, my children. You have been caught in the nets of Christ without realizing it. Tell me now, is it not true that the greatest event in the history of a soul is precisely the event of its being given over to Christ? Is not the greatest celebration for the soul the cherubic *Alleluia* when it is sung with all one's heart? Tell me, did not that Father of the Church speak truly when he wrote: "So beautiful and so good is the monastic life, so truly beautiful and good"?

As you are hastening now to put on the monastic habit, you are in reality hastening to put on Christ. Do not abandon Christ, then, with whom we are going to clothe you. Do not let him escape from your hands if you have not been filled with his presence.

Each of you has made your soul a many-voiced, harmonious harp that plays only for him. Through your contribution, our Brotherhood becomes a divine choir that sings praises to God. Let it be an intervention of divine power of which the Church can be proud. God perceived your spiritual thirst and came running to you. God saw the sacred desires of your hearts and responded. Glorify God, therefore! Magnify the Holy One!

The shepherds saw the Lord as an Infant in the manger and worshiped him. The three disciples on Mount Tabor saw only a flash of God's Glory and fell prostrate, not being able to face his Light. Paul felt the Lord's Presence and was blinded. The aged Prophet saw the Infant in his Mother's arms and asked to die, because he felt that his purpose in life had been fulfilled. For what else can we live, if not to see Christ?

Bow your heads before the very God. Hide beneath God's shadow. Humble yourselves. Disappear, so that the Lord can be magnified. All, all of you, my friends and friends of the Bridegroom Christ, behold the mystery! Marvel at the union that will now take place. Bend your knees before the fearful oaths that you will now hear. They will be spoken by young lips, they will come from young hearts, they will ascend to heaven. History will record them. God himself will sign them. Let us be ecstatic, therefore, with nothing earthly in our thoughts. God, our Lord, is before us!

Father Paisios
and Archimandrite Vasileios

The journey itself to the Holy Mountain had been an exciting experience. The plane trip to Salonica was easy enough. The governmental red tape would have been wholly exasperating if it had not been for the gracious hospitality of Father Vasileios, the pastor of the Cathedral of Aghia Sophia, and his sons. The early-morning bus ride across Khalkidhiki through the mountains was beautiful, although it was already exceedingly warm and humid. The recently developed port at Ouranoupolis, by the medieval tower that once belonged to Vatopedi, retains its charm, and one senses the nearness of the Holy Mountain. But it is the boat ride through the crystalline blue of the Aegean along the rocky coast that finally brings the majestic summit of Athos into view. O Holy Mountain! It is that. It lifts one's spirit up to the ethereal blue and beyond. The good vibrations of a holy place pervade the air and wash away all the frenetic agitation of the secular world. Not even the rumbling old bus, kicking up clouds of hot dust as it climbs toward the capital, disturbs the prevailing sense of peace. More red tape and finally the coveted diamonitirion,* the key to all the monasteries on the Holy Mountain. As the bus rattles down the northern slope toward Iviron, I alight at the turn-off to Stavronikita.

A sign at the entrance road warns the visitor: NO ROOMS, GUESTHOUSE UNDER REPAIR. I clutch my letter of introduction a little tighter and go down the mountain trail, trusting in its ability to find me a monk's cell in the midst of the brothers.

There is obvious surprise on the face of the brother porter as I approach the entryway of the fortresslike monastery. But the greeting is cordial and I am led into Vespers as my letter is taken off to the Hegumen. As we merge at the end of the Service, Father Vasileios is in the coutyard to greet me. A younger man than I expected, with dark complexion and eyes, made darker by his jet-black beard. The brightness of his smile seems to be emphasized by this dark framing. And what light comes from those smiling eyes! The welcome is warm. There will be time to talk after supper. Now it is time to ascend to the refectory.

The meal is quite simple: cold pasta, feta, salad, grapes, and water. While we eat, one of the monks reads, from a volume of Migne, a homily of Saint John Chrysostom. After the rather long thanksgiving the monks descend to the terrace to enjoy the cool evening breeze while the novices clear the tables, wash the dishes, and take the garbage to the chickens cooped out at the end of the interior garden. The view from this terrace is considered one of the finest on the peninsula. The eye reaches out across the northern sea to nearby Iviron Monastery, with its long wharf, then up the hillside to Philotheou and the surrounding sketes, mostly hidden in the luxuriant foliage, and finally sweeps up the gray, treeless granite to the lofty peak of Athos, which seems to be almost detached and weightless as it assumes the pink and golden hues of the reclining sun and is gently embraced by the passing clouds. One's spirit rushes up, so drawn that one feels lightsome, and there is the expectation of momentary transfiguration. Tabor, set by Galilee's shores, is hardly more enthralling than this Holy Mountain.

After responding to the momentary needs of some of his sons and exchanging a few pleasantries with others, Father Vasileios, with a radiant, joyful smile, invited me to join him in the library. It seemed indeed dark after the evening glow on the terrace. There was a large window, but it looked out into the inner court, and the small katholicon pressed close. The rather large room was very full. Except for the round table near the door, stuffed bookshelves seemed to occupy every available space. As Father took his seat at the table, I observed on the shelves immediately behind him the volumes of J.P. Migne's *Patrologia Latina* and *Graeca*. And beside them, the complete *Sources*

Chrétiennes from Paris. Father would eventually comment on this series.

Of all the Hegumens on the Holy Mountain, Father Vasileios is perhaps the one most familiar with Western monasticism. During his studies in Paris and pastoral work in Belgium, he had taken part in ecumenical meetings that sometimes took him to Catholic monasteries. Father insisted that even though our lives are similar in their round of daily worship and work, the spirit with which we live them is quite different. His keen theological mind reached to a root of this difference. Father felt that the Western image of the Church, influenced so heavily by the philosophical concept of a perfect society, with its structures and laws, destroys the mystery. The constant communion with the heavenly realm as forming one Church with us radiates the whole life and space of the Orthodox monastery, and above all its katholicon and the Services celebrated therein. The almost sensible presence, truly visible to the sensitive inner eyes of the faithful, of the awesome Divine energies of the Transcendent Trinity and the Transfigured Christ bring about the deification of the devout and vigilant monk and of the holy community.

We monks and nuns of the East and the West have to be faithful each to our own tradition. And yet we must change so that we can be truly united. But that change must be in the depths. There we must become fire. How? By letting ourselves become enflamed by the Holy Mysteries and by the Holy Fathers and Mothers.

Here at Stavronikita the daily Liturgy is very central. There are only three priests, so Father Vasileios celebrates most days when he is home. And he does it with great depth and care. There is no rush in his prayer. The Mystery is allowed to unfold slowly and fully and to flow through his person and out through all the community.

The Holy Fathers and Mothers, too, are fire. Father acknowledged with gratitude the work done by the Western scholars and publishers in making the texts of the Greek as well as the Latin Fathers so readily available. But he noted how the extensive notes in *Sources Chrétiennes* were very extrinsic. Scientific work does need to be done — but the Fathers and Mothers are fire and we must let ourselves be set afire by them. Each young monk or nun should be guided by his

Elder in the Father or Mother that is best for him. Some of the more simple cannot follow a master such as Saint John Chrysostom, but the more educated need this strong meat.

It was time for Apodeipnon. We gathered in the *liti*, or outer part of the small church, which was now wholly dark except for the two lamps before the principal icons and the reader's light. The splendid poetry of the Acathist Hymn* was softly chanted in honor of the Holy Mother of God, the undisputed Mistress of the Garden of Athos. At the end, each venerated the holy icons, kissed the Hegumen's hand, receiving his blessing, and filed out into the night silence. I collected my bag at the gate just before it was closed for the night and was led to a cell on the second floor. The full moon now made a path across the sea, and its light climbed the two-hundred-foot palisade to silver my balcony and trace a slowly moving pattern on my rough wooden floor. For a time, the murmur of the sea below was accompanied by the murmur of voices in Father Gregorios' cell, next door. But these soon gave way to the overwhelming peace of a night settled deep in the caring love of God.

The semantron sounded at one-thirty to rouse the monks for an hour of prayer in the cell before its second call gathered them in the katholicon. Incense, a quiet chant, a prayer deep and palpable enfolded us as the Midnight Service led into Orthros, and the First and Third Hours into Liturgy. We emerged from the church near seven and soon were summoned to the refectory for "lunch" (fish, potatoes, salad, feta, grapes, and water).

After the meal, Father Vasileios asked his assistant, Father Gregorios, to take me to visit their Spiritual Father, Father Paisios. The day was already warm and humid, and Father set a brisk pace first up the road and then along an almost invisible trail, till we came, after a half hour's time, to what amounted to little more than an enlarged shack with corrugated roof. Father Paisios greeted us warmly. He is a small, lean, graying man who looked much older than his forty-nine years. While we prayed for a bit in the small, plain chapel with its screen of modernized icons, Father prepared the usual sweets, cold water from the well, coffee, and figs. We sat outside the cell on stones that Father had covered with cardboard for us.

I began to ask Father about his life. "I do not remember. I am an idiot." He obviously did not want to speak about himself, so I asked for a word on continual prayer. This was more to his liking. Gently he began: First, you must find a certain inner tranquility and simplicity of life, to be free for prayer and to know yourself. Secondly, you must know the mercy of God. Thirdly, you must realize that prayer is not a burden, but a resting. If you want to pray continually you must free yourself from responsibilities. (Father himself had had his spiritual son, Father Vasileios, named Hegumen of Stavronikita so that he could withdraw to this hermitage and spend his nights and days in prayer.) If one cannot free himself, he should seek to further the possibility for others, and thus he will share in the merit of their prayer. If a monk feels the call to constant prayer, he should be insistent with his superiors to be free, but in the end he must obey. The superior has the responsibility before God. The worst thing is a superior who does not appreciate prayer.

A beginner can have illusions. He can be seeking mystical experience for the wrong reasons. First we must learn our need to seek the mercy of God. If a dirty ragamuffin seeks to snuggle up close to a king, he will be quickly repulsed. But if he shyly peaks out from a distance, he will be summoned, cleaned up, and then welcomed close. As Father recounted this little parable, he acted it out with the greatest simplicity, first pushing away the imaginary child, then crouching down and peeking at us over the extended sleeve of his rhason, and finally rocking in his bosom the little one, his own face suffused with tenderness and joy. No doubt he knew what it is to be rocked in the arms of God.

There were many other things we spoke of. With great emphasis, repeating the word several times, Father urged that we "disorganize" our life in the monastery. We must leave all regimentation behind in order to find spiritual freedom. At Stavronikita after the morning Services the monks are free till Vespers. Each has certain chores he can do when and how it best suits his rhythm. Otherwise his life unfolds under the guidance of the Spiritual Father according to his spiritual needs. But, Father insisted, even the monk who enjoys continual prayer should have his canon (rule) of prayer for the Church, benefactors, et cetera. After this is fulfilled, he is free. Father spoke especially of metanias (prostrations) and prayer on the rope — the cord of knotted beads used when praying the Jesus Prayer. I noted that Father' own knuckles were callused and his thumbs broad and flat, the result of the innumerable prostrations that filled his nights before the icons. Father admitted that reading is important, especially at first, but practice is more so: "Be a philosopher (a lover of true wisdom) not only in spirit but also in life."

During the summer, Father receives many visitors at his hermitage. He is venerated far and wide as one of the holiest monks on the Mountain today. A Bishop in Crete told me how the people in Crete revere him and how the Bishop had repeatedly urged him to come to Crete to bless his people. But Father's reply was always the same: He was no priest, he was unlearned, he had nothing to bring — so he would stay at home.

A novice, who was about to leave the monastery to complete his exams at the university and fulfill his compulsory military service, arrived to seek Father's blessing. He bore a large basket of fruit and vegetables from the monastery garden. In this way, they care for Father's needs. On Saturdays and on the eve of great feasts, Father comes to the monastery to join the Brothers at the Agripnia (the All-night Vigil), at which he takes delight in leading in the singing of the Alleluias with his sweet, strong voice. Such would be the occasion of my next meeting with Father, when I visited this monastery for the Feast of Pentecost, several years later. At that time he would speak more of his service as a Spiritual Father and end by urging me to enter more and more into the Light — for it is there that we will find true unity.

As we left, Father went part way with us. He gave me a small plaque he had made with an impression of the Holy Mountain with its many monasteries and the Holy Mother of God hovering over them. I kissed his hand, so marked by the labors of prayer, and went on ahead while Father Gregorios prostrated to receive the special blessing of this saintly man whom he had the privilege of calling his Father in God.

We returned to the monastery hot and tired but spiritually refreshed. After washing up and resting a bit I found Father Vasileios on the terrace, sitting under the arbor, enjoying what little breeze stirred in the afternoon heat. Still deeply moved by the experience of my morning visit, I thanked Father for arranging it and shared some of my impressions. Father Vasileios insisted that the way to unity is for monks to live truly spiritual lives and become true theologians, like Father Paisios. Father Vasileios is himself a well-educated theologian, highly respected in both East and West. At the Pan-Orthodox Theological Conference in Athens in preparation for the coming Synod it was Father who gave the keynote address. At the Pan-Orthodox Assembly of Youth at Dijon it was Father who summoned the future leaders of the Church to hope and vision. Yet with Evagrius Ponticus, he insisted: "The theologian is the man who prays. And the man who prays is a theologian." The deeper one enters into the Spirit the more he seeks and sees the truth.

Father emphasized the importance of the whole man entering into prayer. The body must take part and become tired. Father was opposed to Christians using Yoga or Zen techniques, which are associated with other cultures and cults that Father saw as having something of the devil in them. Such techniques cannot be wholly divorced from their origins. "Why not use our own, Christian tradition of metanias?" asked Father. For beginners he usually prescribes fifty full prostrations and five komvoschinions (the prayer cord used to count the recitation of the Jesus Prayer), making the little metania with each careful recitation of the Prayer.

Like Father Paisios, Father stressed the importance of freedom in the monastery. Certainly each should have his work to do. Here they are usually assigned about four hours of this a day. Liturgy is celebrated daily, and all are expected to attend. On Saturdays all usually receive the Eucharist. On other days, one receives with the particular blessing of the Father.

For reading, Father especially recommended Saint Isaac the Syrian. He seems to have had the greatest influence on Father and also on Father Paisios. However, Father added a gentle warning in regard to Isaac's eremitical orientation. Nonetheless he found Isaac's teaching to be fully developed, very current and alive, and completely balanced psychologically. He also encouraged the reading of Saint John Climacus (his famous *Ladder*), Saint Symeon the New Theologian, and Saint Gregory Palamas. Although Evagrius is generally unacceptable among Orthodox because of his condemnation for Origenism, he is yet influential, being introduced under other names, such as Saint Nilos.

The day had quickly passed. It was time for Vespers, supper, Apodeipnon, and then another night filled with silence and prayer. Stavronikita is one of the keys to the current renewal that is taking place on the Holy Mountain, as young monks gather around this young Elder so filled with the wisdom that belongs to mature years, so radiant with the joy and light that come from Tabor. Eyes can shine with such love and heavenly mirth only when they are the eyes of one whose inner vision has rested frequently and long on the One Who is Love and the Joy of all the saints.

On the morrow it was time for me to take my leave — all too soon — and to continue on my pilgrimage around the Holy Mountain. After a breakfast of tea and bread, jam and olives, I packed my shoulder bag and prepared to set out along the coast toward Iviron Monastery. Father Vasileios was waiting for me at the top of the descent to the sea. We exchanged a few brief words that tried to bear the weighty message of an experienced depth of communion. Father gave me a small carved icon of the Holy Virgin as she appears on the iconostasis of the Protaton.* I went to kneel to receive his fatherly blessing, but he pulled me to my feet and we exchanged the triple kiss of brotherhood. As I walked slowly down the hill past the cemetery chapel, I knew I would return. And each return, each meeting with this holy Father would be a blessing.

CONFERENCE OF ARCHIMANDRITE VASILEIOS

*Given at the Pan-Orthodox Youth Congress
Dijon, France, November 1974*

One of the Fathers says, "As for me, I am not a monk, but I have seen real monks." This saying helps me and justifies my presence among you this evening. From what I have seen, I shall try to say a few words about what an Orthodox monk is, and about the profound relationship we all have with the liturgical life of the monasteries and with the personal experiences of those who are truly living the monastic life.

The Lord Jesus did not come into the world merely to make an improvement in our present conditions of life. Neither did he come to put forward an economic or political system, nor to teach a method of arriving at a psychosomatic equilibrium.

He came to conquer death and to bring us eternal life. "God so loved the world that he gave his only begotten Son to the end that all who believe in him should not perish but have eternal life." And this eternal life is not a promise of happiness beyond space and time, not a mere survival after death or a prolongation of our present life. Eternal life is the Grace of God, which here and now illuminates and gives sense to things present and to things to come, both to body and soul, to the human person in its entirety.

The appearances of the Risen Lord to his disciples had the purpose of filling them with the certainty that death had been overcome. Christ is risen. "Death has no more dominion over him." He is Perfect God, who goes in and out, the doors being shut. He is perfect man, who can be touched, who eats and drinks like any one of his disciples.

What makes us truly human and gives us our specific value is not our physical or intellectual capacities but the grace of having a share in the Resurrection of Christ, of being able, from now on, to live and die Eternal Life. "Whoever loves his life will lose it; but whoever hates his life in this world will keep it unto life eternal." The monk, with the total gift of himself to God, saves the one unique truth. He lives the one unique joy. "Whoever loses his life in this world, will save it." The life of the monk is thus a losing and a finding.

The Orthodox monk is not what one is accustomed to call a "mystic." He is not someone who by employing certain abstinences or techniques has arrived at a high degree of self-control or at various ascetic exploits. All these things are only realizations belonging to this present world, unimportant in themselves, incapable of overcoming death, either for the monk or for his brothers and sisters.

The true Orthodox monk is one who has "seen the Resurrection of the Lord," who has "received something of the experience of the Resurrection." He is man raised up.

His mission is not to effect something by his thought or to organize something by his own capacities but by his life to give his witness to the conquest of death. And this he does only by burying himself like a grain of wheat in the earth.

This is why, in the *Sayings of the Fathers*, when a young monk said to his Spiritual Father, "I see that my mind is constantly with God," his Spiritual Father replied, "It is no great thing that your mind should be with God; what matters is that you should feel yourself lower than all creation." In this way the old man helped the young monk to transport himself into a different realm. From a partial preoccupation with his own thoughts about God, he invited him to the total offering of himself, to a humbling that is a true death, and at the same time a resurrection into a new life, humble but all-powerful.

In the university of the Desert (which is what the Fathers called the monastic life) the monks not only learn the things of God, they live them and suffer them. They not only tire their minds and their bodies; they sacrifice their whole self. "Unless I have destroyed everything, I shall not be able to build myself up."

The true monk is one who has been raised from the dead, a first fruit of the general resurrection, an image of the Risen Christ. He shows that the immaterial is not necessarily spiritual and that the bodily is not necessarily fleshly. Everything that has been sanctified by the mystery of the Cross and Resurrection (whether material or immaterial) is spiritual, that is, everything that has been transfigured by the uncreated Divine Energies.

Thus the monk reveals the spiritual mission of what is created and bodily. At the same time, he reveals the tangible existence of what is uncreated and immaterial. The monk is one who is wholly dedicated to this mystery. He has the sacred task of celebrating, in the midst of the Orthodox Church, the salvation of all created things. In a particular way, he is concerned with all and concerned with nothing, "separated from all and united with all." The ideal of specialization is foreign to his very nature. He is not specialized in one thing and unconcerned about something else. Everything concerns him.

What does have meaning for him, what enlightens him and shows him his real concern is the way in which each thing is situated, integrated, ordered, finds its true place and its true beauty within the transfigured universe, within the Divine Liturgy of the salvation of all things. This revelation and this knowledge of the principle of coherence in all things does concern the monk. This principle relates to all things. For this reason, whatever has been transfigured, whatever has participated wholly in the Divine Energy which saves all things, concerns him equally. All this helps him to know himself and to know whatever he encounters.

A monk has written, "It is not my job to build houses or to whitewash them. Nor is it my job to read and write. What is my calling? It is, if possible, to die in God. Then I shall live and be moved by another Power. Then I can do all things freely (dig, organize, read, write), without being attached to anything. I can go everywhere, but wherever I go, I must go seeking for the one thing necessary. I can allow all kinds of trials to come my way, looking always in them for the one thing that makes sense of them all.

"When you build in order to build, you are enlarging your tomb. When you write in order to write, you are weaving your shroud. When you live and breathe seeking always the mercy of God, then an incorruptible garment is woven around you, and you find the sweetness of a heavenly comfort welling up within you. Whether you build or whether you write, that is something altogether secondary."

The monk's purpose in life is not to achieve his individual progress or integration. His purpose is to serve the whole mystery of salvation, by living not for himself but for him who died and rose again for us, and thus for all his brethren.

And this is possible because the monk lives not according to his own will but according to the universal, the catholic will and tradition of the Church.

*   *   *

Monastic tonsure, entry into the monastic life, takes place within the Holy Eucharist.

The postulant offers himself before the Holy Table of Sacrifice. He is admitted as a member of a holy community, a community that is holy because it places its whole life with all its hopes and aspirations on the Table of the Lord, who is himself its sole true Abbot.

Just as it is not the virtue of the priest which transforms the bread and the wine into the Body and Blood of Christ but the grace of the priesthood with which he is invested, so in the life and formation of the monk, it is not basically the capacity of the superior or of the brethren which is at work but the Spirit of Tradition.

In all the Fathers, one can find the same guiding light. All lead to the same end, to the land of liberty of the Spirit. Each one speaks in his own way, expresses his own experience, stresses what he has understood. And from the whole of this Spirit-filled multitude, who have lived in many places and in many countries, there arises a harmonious and single voice, which sings but one hymn before the Throne of the Lamb. This hymn sounds out now and always, it sounds out in the liturgical space of our life, free from the barriers erected by petty human ambitions and social conventions.

Thus the same Power who is above time and full of all goodness, who created all things out of nothing and consecrates the holy gifts upon the altar, and who formed the unanimity of the choir of the Holy Fathers also consecrates the monk, who offers himself to this life, and takes into his Hands the whole development and life of every monastic community.

Our whole life turns around God who is our time and our occupation. Our physical endurance and the first fruits of our mind are offered to God. The Divine Services, study, and prayer constitute the meaning of our struggle and the axis around which we turn. The Eucharistic Liturgy is the heart of our organism, and itself builds up our personal life and our community of brothers.

From the architectural point of view, the monastery has been constructed to serve the Divine Liturgy. One could say that the whole building is the Liturgy sung in stone. Around the church, like cherubim and seraphim, the galleries and cells, the refectory and the library are gathered to form a single whole, the space in which the Liturgy is carried forward throughout the twenty-four hours of the day.

Everything has its own place in the liturgical ordering of things. This is why, following the rhythm of the monastery's life, walking through its passages, one has the impression of constantly turning around the one thing necessary. One turns with one's thoughts and one's work, one's grief and one's joy, one's body and one's soul, caught up in the Divine Liturgy of the whole life of the community, which it offers on behalf of the whole world.

One could say that the whole life and construction of the monastery are nothing but a living icon of the Risen Christ. By his Resurrection, Christ has destroyed the gates of death, and in calm triumph he has raised up to salvation Adam and all those who were in bondage. In the same way, the holy Liturgy raises up all our lives into the kingdom of heaven, and the monastic church lifts up all the buildings of the monastery toward the light and peace of sanctification. The rhythm of death and resurrection, which is characteristic of this way of life, spreads to all things. All true joy and all true consolation both in Orthodoxy and in Orthodox monasticism come through death.

True consolation is nothing other than the passage through death into every form of life. We can see this in the long monastic Services, in the fasts, and in the whole practice of the ascetic life. Are these Orthodox rules hard? Are they austere? Do they go beyond human endurance? It looks like that from outside. It is so, in part at least, in reality. "The life of the monk is a violence against nature," says Saint

John Climacus. But these struggles are never despairing, however hard they may seem. They are never stifling or contrary to our true nature, even though they may seem dark. Because in the end, in the midst of much labor, of ascesis and vigils that often do go beyond human endurance, a shoot comes to birth, a shoot of new and unfading life which gives fruit a hundredfold. And then you bless all pains and sufferings. You sacrifice all things, because the joy that has appeared is a gleam of the age to come, which gives light and life both to the present and to the future. Thus spontaneously you come to search what is harder, more somber, more lonely, in order to go forward toward this true consolation, which does not deceive, toward this light that does not set but makes us able to communicate with all others and with all things.

Those who are truly monks arrive at the point of accepting gladly and with thanksgiving both grief and pain and the contempt and humiliation of men, because they have been freed from the deceitful pleasures of this world and share already, here and now, in the eternal glory of their Lord. Saint Symeon the New Theologian tells us, "I reckoned the temptations and the troubles that came to me as nothing in comparison not with the future but with the present glory of our Lord Jesus Christ."

*   *   *

Here is something very characteristic. An old monk, a true ascetic, comes to our monastery from time to time to ask for a little help. With what he receives, he feeds himself and also helps others, older than himself.

One day he came for his usual visit and said to one of the brethren of the monastery, "I hope I am not being too much trouble to you, coming and asking for your help. If I am too much bother, don't worry yourself, I needn't come again. Don't worry about it. A monk is like a dog; if you give him a kick, that does him good, and if you don't give him a kick but a piece of bread instead, that does him good as well."

This old man, although he is more than seventy-five, doesn't expect anyone to respect him. He thinks of himself as a dog. He bows to all and asks their blessing, not only to the monks but also to the novices and to the pilgrims who come to us. But he is full of such inexpressible grace that a kind of wave of joy runs through the monastery every time he comes. All of us, monks and pilgrims, gather around him to hear the words of grace that come from his lips, to be encouraged by the joy his face reflects without his ever suspecting it. He is like that Father of the Desert who asked God that he might not receive any glory on this earth, and whose face was so radiant that no one could look straight at him.

In humble persons like this, who radiate grace, one feels that the two great virtues are always at work: the mystery of repentance and the mystery of love. They are not persons who have been converted, who have repented. They are those who are being converted, who are repenting. The Lord's call to repentance does not mean that we are to be converted once only, nor that we should repent from time to time (though one ought to begin with that). It means that our whole life should be a conversion, a constant repentance; that in us there should always be a state of repentance and contrition. We ought not to speak, or think, or do anything outside that atmosphere, that attitude of penitence and contrition which should fill our whole being with profound humility.

At every moment this mystery of penitence, of contrition, of being raised up by the power of Another, should be at work in us. At every moment, being cast down, we feel ourselves to be raised up by Another. We feel that we are fallen and he is the Resurrection, that we are non-being, and he is Being itself. It is by his Infinite Grace that he brings us from non-being to Being. When we were fallen God raised us up, and he does raise us up at every moment. Thus as the spirit of repentance grows within us, we are led to say with the Apostle, "I carry in my body the dying of the Lord Jesus, that the life of the Lord Jesus may also be manifest in our body." These true monks live at one and the same time Good Friday and Easter Sunday. They constantly live the "life-giving death" of the Lord, the "sorrow that brings joy."

Their sense of repentance is equaled by their sense of the Divine Charity. In love they see the way of sacrifice, which leads directly and surely to eternal life. No effort that is offered for love of God remains in vain. Everything offered and given up for love of the brethren is saved, kept intact, multiplied in eternal life.

Our neighbor is not simply an indispensable companion on the way of life. Our neighbor is an integral part of our spiritual existence. Only in losing ourselves for God and for one another can we find the true dimension of our life. "Whoever loses . . . finds." Only thus is the grandeur that comes from God restored to us. Only in this way can we feel within ourselves that the foundations on which we build are unshaken. These foundations are loss of self according to the Gospel, death in Christ. The anthropological reality in which the new person lives from henceforth is the Divine Grace that embraces all things.

The reward given for the glass of water offered to our brother or sister is the new trinitarian consciousness that comes to birth within us. The other one is no longer the frontier that determines our individuality, closes off our own living space, or simply flatters our vanity. The other is not the shroud that envelops our deadly isolation. The other is not hell. The other is the true place of our life, my most dear and irreplaceable self, who gives me, here and now, through my gift of myself, the meaning and reality of eternal life, an eternal life that has already begun. As the Beloved Disciple says, "We know that we have passed from death to life, because we love one another."

*   *   *

Coming into contact with a monk who has reached maturity, one finds nothing superhuman in him, nothing that astonishes or makes one giddy but, rather, something deeply human and humble, something that brings peace and new courage. Despite his ascesis, despite his separation from the world, he is not in reality cut off from others. On the contrary, he has returned to them, he has embraced all persons in their suffering, and he has become truly human.

Progress in the monastic life is not reckoned by the quantity of fasting and bodily penance but by the degree to which each monk has been led to become a partaker of the Grace of the Comforter, to be open to the Spirit, and thus to be at peace in himself in such a way as to *be* peace for all his brothers and sisters.

The monks of a certain community who were full of the thought that by reason of their constant recitation of the Jesus Prayer they were surpassing other monks in virtue, received this word from a Spiritual

Father. "Do not tell me how often you say the komvoschinion, how many times you repeat the Prayer. It's something else that interests me. Is there anyone among you, even the most advanced, who can understand the tired mankind of our own day, who can comfort those who suffer? Is there anyone who can free those who have fallen into the snares of the enemy? If there is such a one who can give peace to his brother and sister, who can enable them to come to love life, to rejoice and be thankful to God, that will show that there are monks among you who have made spiritual progress."

This attitude of this Spiritual Father of Mount Athos is very characteristic. It shows to what degree the life of the true monk involves love for others. It measures all by the measures of love, by the salvation of all, not by the imaginary activity of each one separately.

The light that shines from the genuine monk is a light that reveals. It resembles the presence of Christ. "If they say to you, he is in the desert, go not out; if they say he is in the secret place, believe them not; for as the lightning shines from the East to the West, so shall the coming of the Son of Man be." The monk does not say do this or do that, in a human way; he does not propose his own plans or express his own opinions. Rather, he pours out strength and comfort. In his presence, one feels peace and security. Near him, everything is filled with light. Uncertainties vanish; one begins to love Christ, and to love life. One no longer fears death.

Such monks, unknown and anonymous but full of light, exist. I know one. He literally overflows. That is an expression that gives some idea of the truth about him.

He has a treasure of inexpressible joy hidden in an earthen vessel, small and fragile. And this joy overflows and spreads all around him, filling his surroundings with its fragrance. Light shines from his being. His inner rejoicing sometimes goes beyond his endurance, breaks his heart, shows itself in tears and cries and gestures. And whether he speaks or whether he is silent, whether he sleeps or whether he is awake, whether he is present or whether he is absent, it is always the same thing he says, the same thing he is, the same grace and the same power. His presence or its memory, the feeling that he is near or simply that he exists, of itself conveys something other, something uncreated, tranquil, penetrating. It is something that renews us, calms our nerves, extinguishes our anger, enlightens our heart and mind, gives wings to our hope, and prepares us for a struggle that gives quiet and peace to a whole people.

Here something that is before all ages and unmoved is constantly coming to birth. That which emanates from him can neither be exhausted not fragmented. For in each part, each fragment, the mystery of the whole is found, and this whole is unbroken, something other, something new, seen and heard for the first time. To each one, he says the same thing, and each one is able to find in him what he seeks, what he needs. It is not what he says which is important but the spirit that animates it. It is the Spirit which nourishes heart and tongue, gives form to his sayings, and transforms the stones of his speech into icons.

He is an instrument, a harp of the Spirit, a harp that vibrates in accordance with the lightest breath of the Spirit. This is why the melody that comes from him is fascinating and opens the door into another world; profoundly human, it humanizes us and resolves all our problems. He is a man who has won Paradise with his blood. He has broken open his own person and offers himself to all.

Now he moves untroubled in the midst of all things, in a way unlike that of other people. Everywhere, he finds himself at home, since he has always burnt his own hut for the love of others. Everywhere he places his foot, he finds a rock, because, everywhere, he has humbled himself and let the other pass over him. In all his words he speaks clearly, he finds the image he desires, because he has never deceived anyone, has wounded no one, and has never hurt any creature. He has assuaged the pain of the whole world.

Thus his voice is broken, his breath cut short, his hands and his feet tremble. And yet despite that he stands firm. He sees, he advances, he loves. He is free, a man of the age to come. For this reason he alone speaks justly of this present age.

He is a day of sunshine and of calm; a well of purity and of fruitful virginity. His whole body, as it were, forms a laugh of silent joy. Gentleness and radiance both come from him. Like a day in spring when the breeze is full of scents of new life, so his words are full of the fragrance that comes from the radiant valleys of his heart, the slopes of his sacred and light-bearing reflections.

Near him one becomes pure, is endued with grace by grace. For this man is an icon of theology and of holiness, a revelation of the union of two natures in Christ. Already in this life his body is nourished and preserved by the experience of the Spirit. The heavenly manna feeds his body, fills his heart, strengthens his bones.

In the words of the Divine Liturgy, he knows God, who is at once terrible and the lover of us all. He is weak, delicate indeed, and yet all-powerful. He receives such a deluge of grace that the house of clay is overwhelmed. His feeble body can no longer endure, he overflows, is on fire, and all within him and around him becomes light. He is an ocean of light, where one can swim all one's life, there where all creation and history find their salvation.

The Uncreated Spirit, who has made its dwelling in his heart gives meaning and substance to the things within him and around him. This Uncreated Spirit is much more tangible, more existing than the landscape around us. And his body is transparent, full of light.

He is nature and holiness, perfect man and perfect God by grace. He does nothing which is false. He does not make things, he causes things to be begotten and to proceed. He does not speak, he acts. He does not comment, he loves.

His thoughts are action, his word creation. His absence fills all things. His presence makes space for all. He has a different conception of life, of the world, of distances.

He does not exist in the world, and at the same time he recapitulates it, gives it form and structure. "By his prayers," as one troparion says, "he established the whole world."

He has gone out of the realm of our habitual actions. If you strike him, your blows will not reach him; he is beyond them. If you seek him, wherever you are, you will find him beside you. He lives only for you.

His image, his life, his voice, his conception of the world emerge at every moment. And this just because his life is constantly hidden, his body lost, his existence spiritualized; his flesh acquires a radiant transparence; all his being is full of immortality.

"I have partaken of the image of God, but not having preserved the image, the Lord has partaken of our flesh in order to save the image and make the flesh immortal."

In his presence, one understands the theology of Saint Gregory Palamas. From the inaccesible essence of his holiness an inexplicable grace constantly and freely comes forth, touching the whole person, body and spirit, like a life-giving light. And just as the sun gives life to all creation, so this light that shines out from the monk gives the possibility of growth to the life of every human being.

This light is not limited, nor is it broken up. It does not create factions or nourish private enthusiasms. It does not organize things in a human fashion. It helps everyone to find his own true self. It helps everyone to love his own life, leading him on in the light that knows no setting.

All confess to the bearer of this light, and he confesses to all. None of us hesitates to reveal the secrets of our hearts to him. On the contrary, we open our heart to him with confidence, as a flower opens toward the sun. And he has no fear that others should learn the secrets of his life. On the other hand, he often places a screen of silence between his burning and luminous being and the feeble senses of his visitors, for fear that the latter should lose their power of seeing ordinary and everyday things at the sight of this blinding splendor. Thus, gently and without noise, he allows the splendor that dwells in him to bring peace and strength, light and joy to those who are his brothers and sisters, the images of God. He does not frighten us with his ascetic exploits but brings us peace by sharing with us the love of God, in which he lives night and day.

In conversation he is attentive and polite. He knows, he sees, he loves. He sees where things are leading. Thus in this atmosphere of a total truth (both for life and for us), he acts. He exposes your difficulties one by one, in the most natural way. You do not suffer from the operation you are undergoing. Another has suffered for you first, Jesus Christ. And now you can find yourself in this place of peace that his sufferings have created for you. "Behold, by the Cross joy has come to the whole world."

He lets you see him, assimilate him, and each time, in the course of conversation, he asks how you feel. You perceive that he is helping you discreetly. He does not interfere harshly. He does not impose himself in some magic way. He shows you how your true self should function according to its nature. He leaves you free. And you find yourself a prisoner of the truth, of freedom, of reality itself. And you go away absolved, without anxieties, made quiet and made strong. You go away and return to your work, you go wherever you like, and yet you always remain here. It is here that you carry the one experience of your life that makes this place a Mount Horeb for you, a place that can be called "God has seen . . . God has been seen." An umbilical cord of hope binds your spiritual being to this place, this moment, this face, this experience. And by this cord the spiritual seed is nourished and developed in the womb of the Church — the new man grows and is born in the Holy Spirit.

In his presence, you feel that the saints of old continue to live among us, since he who is dead to the world lives in another way, in the Holy Spirit, in our midst. He shows us in this way that he, too, will not abandon us. In his presence you feel that you are living in the last time and being judged. It is his love, which you do not deserve, that judges you. His discernment, his piercing eye do not blame. You understand thus how God will judge the world. You understand, too, how the Christian doctrine of the immortality of the soul is to be interpreted, how the resurrection of the body will be. Things present and things to come are made clear not by discursive reasoning but by appearing, being made manifest in life. You find that you are in the presence of an epiphany and a true revelation of the human person.

An eschatological dimension begins already to give fulfillment to your life. The last things begin for you to be filled with a human warmth and hope.

The presence of the saints of old becomes evident. The grace of those of our own time transcends history and here and now leads us into eternity. Whether they live or whether they die, they bear witness to the power of the Resurrection. They reveal our fundamental dignity and the unending light of the Kingdom for which we were created. They show us that there is no difference between the old and the new in the Church, which is the body of the Risen Christ, "Who makes all things new."

A young monk has written about a Spiritual Father of an earlier time:

I am reading Saint Isaac. I find something true, heroic, spiritual in him; something which transcends space and time. I feel that for the first time, here is a voice which resonates in the deepest parts of my being, hitherto closed and unknown to me. Although he is so far removed from me in time and space, he has come right into the house of my soul. In a moment of quiet he has spoken to me; sat down beside me. Although I have read so many other things, although I have met so many people, and though today there are others living around me, no one else has been so discerning. To no one else have I opened the door of my soul in this way. Or to put it better, no one else has shown me in such a brotherly, friendly way that there is such a door, a door that opens onto a space that is open and unlimited. And no one else has told me this unexpected and ineffable thing, that the whole of this world belongs to us.

For the first time I feel a holy pride in our human or, better, divine-human nature, an amazement before it. The presence of a saint, separated from the world and from the stain of sin, has given me this divine blessing. He belongs to our human nature. I rejoice at this. I enjoy the benefits of his blessing. Being of the same nature as myself, he really transfuses the life-giving blood of his freedom into me. He shows me myself in my true nature. By his presence he tells me that we are together, and I feel that it is so. This is not something foreign to me. He is himself my most true self. He is an unblemished flower of our human nature.

We may thus conclude by recalling the heartening words of the Prophet Isaiah: "Thus says the Lord, Blessed are those whose roots are in Sion and their kinsfolk in Jerusalem." And indeed, we may all say that we are blessed, because we have our roots in the Mount Sion of Orthodoxy, the holy Mount of Athos, the holy ascetic Fathers; and in the Jerusalem above we have so many kinsfolk. They live for us and constitute the light and hope of our life, present and to come.

Archimandrite Sophrony

Disciple of Father Silouan

Father Sophrony is perhaps best known because of the role he has played in bringing to the West the spiritual wisdom of his own Spiritual Father, the humble monk of Saint Panteleimon, Father Silouan. Indeed, Father Sophrony hides as it were in the shadow of his holy Father and quietly tells the visitor that it is the latter's doctrine that guides life at the little Monastery of Saint John the Baptist in Tolleshunt Knight, Essex. But Father Sophrony himself is undoubtedly a great Spiritual Father.

Father was born in Moscow and left his native land as a consequence of the sorrow and distress the First World War and the revolution brought into his life. As a young artist he went to Paris to study. But there the technical requirements of art school crushed his flowering spirit and he left to seek the freedom of spirit for which his soul thirsted. He went to Mount Athos.

For Father Sophrony this is the essence of monasticism: a life organized to give one the greatest freedom to be unto God. This is why the monk goes apart. The many social activities of ordinary people would deprive him of time and freedom if he had to be involved in them. In the Orthodox tradition there are no laws of enclosure. The people mingle freely with the monks when they come to Saint John the Baptist Monastery. Yet the monk, of his nature, needs to be apart. There is a delicate balance to be found and kept. Freedom is also the reason for the monk's celibacy — not disesteem for marriage. For Father Sophrony, obedience is more important to the monk than celibacy. This opens him to the revelation of God. Knowing his own limitations and blindness, he seeks a spiritual guide and obeys the revelation of God's will through him and through the daily circumstances of life, which the Spiritual Father helps him to interpret.

During his first five years at the Holy Monastery of Saint Panteleimon, on Mount Athos, Father Sophrony had a good Spiritual Father, but better things were to come. In the simple lay monk Father Silouan he was to find the Father who was able to help him solve his spiritual and theological difficulties and enter fully into the ways of the Lord. When he speaks now of his vocation, he says simply that he has no regrets in the choice he made.

Father believes that it is better ordinarily if one's Spiritual Father is also his confessor, who can give him sacramental absolution, and therefore a priest. But this is not essential. Other things are more important. A lay monk can have greater spiritual wisdom. This is the important thing. The ways of prayer and monastic living are not taught much by words but by living example.

For eight years, Father had the privilege of close contact with Father Silouan. Then, in 1938, when his Spiritual Father died, he asked and received his Hegumen's permission to go to the "Desert," to live in solitude on the Holy Mountain. After four years in greater solitude, he moved nearer a monastery and served the community (and three other communities at the request of their respective superiors) as a confessor (Spiritual Father).

After seven years in the Desert, in response to constant requests Father consented to undertake to write of Father Silouan and prepare the deceased Father's writings for publication. For this he came to Paris. He had hoped it would be for a year only, but the task proved a long one. While he labored at it, disciples came to him in Paris. As he had no place to accommodate them, they lived in scattered quarters in the city but hoped that one day they could live together. There was no precise design to found a monastery, only a desire to be together with their Spiritual Father.

In 1959 they heard of an abandoned vicarage in Tolleshunt Knight, in Essex, near the east coast of England. The Anglican Church and the local people were willing to let them use it. And thus they came to England, Father Sophrony and four disciples. At the time of my

visit, one of these had left, but two others had come. I know best Father
Symeon, a Swiss convert from Calvinism, who joined Father in Paris.
After some years of monastic life, Father Sophrony sent him back to
Paris to get his degree in theology. Father Sophrony believes monks
should be well educated if they have the aptitude and attraction for it,
but only after a solid monastic formation. First they must learn to pray.
Then they will come to desire a fuller dogmatic formation, and that is
the time for studies. There is a relatively young monk in the community (coming from Sydney, he was the only one in the community who
spoke English as his native tongue; it is a very "catholic" community,
coming from many countries, speaking many languages) who had
been sent to Paris, to Saint Sergius, to study theology for over five
years.

I asked Father about the selection and training of candidates.

On principle, all who come asking admission are admitted; that
is, all Orthodox or converts to Orthodoxy. Father sees the Liturgy to
be so at the heart of the life of the monastic community that he believes
it unwise to admit an Anglican or a Roman Catholic to the community,
though they are welcome to come and to pray with the community.

The newcomer is simply brought into the life of the family. I was
very agreeably surprised to discover how much Father saw the
monastic community as a family, close, warm, intimate, fully sharing
— though Father did not hesitate to warn against an undesirable
emotionalism. This family spirit was nowhere more evident than in
the refectory.

The family at Saint John the Baptist had an unusual enrichment.
Some women came desiring the monsastic life. As there were no other
possibilities at the moment, they were allowed to live in a house on the
property. In time, they would have their own convent. They came to
Liturgy, Services (this added much to the beauty of the singing), and
refectory, staying always on the left side. And they were permitted to
use the library. There were three nuns in all. One was a professor of
philosophy in France, another was a Danish psychiatrist. And then
there was Father Elias' mother, who sat at Father Sophrony's left in the
refectory. With regal dignity, she seemed to preside with him as the
mother of the community.

Father admitted there were problems having the nuns there, and there were advantages, especially for receiving women guests. Double monasteries are not unheard of in the tradition. Saint Basil himself provided for nun's monasteries to be close by those of the monks, but they were distinctly separate. England knew genuine double monasteries in the Middle Ages, with Gilbert of Springham, and earlier, when great abbesses ruled both men and women.

Father is the spiritual guide of all at Saint John's. He sees that the guidance to be given is essentially the same for all, but there are differences. One can be more severe with men. With women, severity can more easily lead to despair, so greater care must be taken. Yet one must be firm. And the emotions must be watched.

In the family atmosphere of the community the newcomer learns to pray. There are no techniques. The emphasis is on the liturgical prayer and the Prayer of Jesus. As the small community has to work hard to gain its living, there are only two Services on workdays (each of which might last two hours), one at six in the morning, the other at six in the evening. On Sundays and feasts, the monks might spend up to twelve hours in church. The Eucharistic Liturgy is ordinarily celebrated only three times a week: Saturday, Sunday, and Tuesday, the day dedicated to Saint John the Baptist. (In the Orthodox tradition each day has its special dedication: Monday, all the Angelic Powers; Tuesday, Saint John the Baptist; Wednesday and Friday, the Holy Cross; Thursday, Saints Peter and Paul; Saturday, all the Company of the Blessed, all the faithful departed.)

For reading, Father recommends to the young, first, Dorotheus of Gaza. Then John of the Ladder (Climacus). But, Father adds, John is not easy. He writes concisely and presumes in his illustrations a knowledge of the times, for he speaks familiarly of current things, just as we might say: "I'll phone you." (For an elderly man, born in the nineteenth century, who only began to learn English in 1959, Father does remarkably well. He spent a month at Crowley-Down with the Anglican monks in order to learn the language.) Then there are John Cassian, Barsanuphius (Dorotheus' Spiritual Father), and John. Afterward Father recommends Isaac the Syrian and, of course, the *Philokalia*. Father thinks the *Art of Prayer* excellent, having the true spirit of the *Philokalia* but more concrete, a better text to begin with. He also recommends Archbishop Ignatius Brianchaninov's *The Arena: an Offering to Contemporary Monasticism.*

The newcomer is always free to leave. But if he decides to stay, it is also primarily he who decides when he will make his profession as a monk. This decision must also be made by Father as the Spiritual Father. In addition, as the Superior of the Monastery, he will consult the brethren on their feelings about living with this brother.

*   *   *

I had several reasons for wanting to visit Father Sophrony. I knew it would be an occasion of grace to meet the holy monk. I wanted to see if we could reprint his book on Father Silouan, *The Undistorted Image.* And I wanted to consult him on the symposium that was being planned, to be held at Oxford in September 1973. The theme was "the Cistercians and the Spiritual Tradition of the Christian East," an ecumenical symposium bringing together Cistercians and Orthodox. The papers and reports from this symposium have been published in *One Yet Two* (Kalamazoo, Michigan: Cistercian Publications, 1976).

I had heard that it would be difficult to get to see Father, so I called Father Symeon, whom I had met two years earlier at Orval, a Cistercian abbey in southern Belgium. He responded most warmly and graciously, gave full directions on how to reach Tolleshunt Knight, and promised to be at the bus to meet us. I started out early in the morning with a young Carthusian monk from Saint Hugh's Charterhouse.

True to his word, Father Symeon was there when we stepped down from our bus. After a hearty handshake, Father insisted on carrying my bag as we walked down the road to the old "Vicarage." I was surprised how much he remembered of our former meeting. And he was immediately interested in our plans for the symposium.

When we reached the monastery, Father took us to the chapel and left us to pray before the icons while he announced our arrival to Father Sophrony. Father Sophrony came immediately. He shook my hand vigorously in silence. And then, very significantly, as if to express a desire to share all with us, his greatest treasures, he drew aside the sanctuary curtain, opened the Holy Doors, and began to pray the Our

Father. After this shared prayer, we went to his room, and Father Symeon went to bring coffee and cookies.

For over an hour, Father Sophrony answered fully all the questions we put to him and listened attentively to all we said. He had asked Father Symeon to stay. And I was impressed how this monk, himself a true man of the spirit and a recognized theologian, listened attentively to his Spiritual Father and spoke only when invited to do so. I was wishing that we could have a tape recorder to catch all that Father said to us. But as my companion truly observed, so much of it was the man speaking and the way he spoke. In appearance, Father Sophrony is just what you would expect a wise, holy *Abba* to look like. But there was a certain childlike eagerness that brought immense life into his shining eyes and gently wrinkled face. He often fingered the silver cross that hung around his neck on a simple chain. His habit was but a plain black robe. His gray-black hair and beard, which he sometimes gently tugged, were moderately long. At times he leaned back in his chair, listening attentively or speaking slowly and quietly; at other times he leaned eagerly over his desk, and on a couple occasions struck it with his hand.

I noticed the books on his desk. One he showed us was edited by our mutual friend, the Anglican priest, Canon Allchin, entitled *We Belong to One Another*. Father Symeon had written one of the chapters. The other was in French, Mother Gallois' delightful *Life of Little Saint Placid*. On his shelves there was a goodly supply of C.S. Lewis, Knox's *Orthodoxy*, *The Walsingham Way*, *Meister Eckhart*, and much else besides the Fathers of the East and of the West. The walls were covered with icons, including one immense one of Mary with the Child that Father himself had painted. When he has time, he helps one of his monks who does beautiful iconography in a shop behind the monastery. This monk had studied art in Paris.

When the first bell rang, we broke off our dialogue to wash for lunch. I was invited to sit at Father's right. Grace was said in English, beginning with the Lord's Prayer, and Father asked me to give the blessing. It was a simple meal of mashed potatoes, peas, a boiled egg, apple sauce, and coarse brown bread, with water to drink. It began in silence as Father Symeon dished out the portions and Sister served them. Like a loving daughter and sister, she saw that Father Sophrony took his medicine and Father Symeon had his pills and that all got enough to eat. We were introduced to each other around the table, and then there was some reading while we ate, an article from *Faith and Unity*.

After dinner we again went to Father Sophrony's room to continue our many questions. He seemed never to tire of us. I would like to write all he said, but here are a few things that stand out in my mind:

What is imposed has no value for everlasting, eternal life.

Discipline cannot be imposed. It has to come from within a man freely.

There are two different ways. I admire your Western order. But we give more room to the personal development. I think this is more important. I would rather have some disorder and have this.

Individual and personal are very different. Individual (*atom*) is the opposite of unity, it is the most disunited. Personal development leads to unity. It is greatest in Christ, the personal (*hypostasis*) union.

When we achieve freedom in Christ, we come to know the divinity of Christ. In freedom, we really come to know ourselves and our need and how only Christ fills it by his Divinity.

We must be like children and simply accept what the Gospels tell us about Christ.

And how much more did he say, what words of life; they are written in my heart.

All too soon, it was time for us to leave for our bus. That we might have a little more time together and have a cup of coffee, Father asked Father Symeon to drive us to the train. As we were leaving, I went to kneel for Father's blessing, but he would not allow it. He blessed me and give me the kiss of peace in the Orthodox way — kissing my right shoulder, then my left shoulder, then again my right, before embracing me in the style of the West. We drove off with Father Symeon, very happy indeed. And as we parted at the station, Father and I exchanged the kiss of peace.

It was a wonderful and grace-filled experience. Happily it occurred on the final day of the Church Unity Octave, the Feast of Paul's Conversion. I marvel at what the Spirit of the Lord has done in our times. Father Sophrony twice mentioned the fact that Father Silouan "prayed for all humankind." He himself has that universal love. He told us that the English edition of *The Undistorted Image* has only half of his introduction and half of Father Silouan's texts. Father agreed to the rest being translated and the whole published. It is to be hoped that as the holy Monk from Mount Athos becomes better known, he will do much for the healing of the wounds in the Church-Body of Christ. Although he says he has never left the Desert and is as it were a prisoner in this world, I am sure Father Sophrony, as a true Spiritual Father, has a God-given mission to share with us all the spiritual wisdom of his Spiritual Father.

CONFERENCE OF
ARCHIMANDRITE SOPHRONY

To the Monks of the Cistercian Abbey
of Bellefontaine, in France

My Fathers, give me your blessing!

As you know, I have lived on Mount Athos for twenty-two years and I know its monasteries well. Mount Athos is a peninsula inhabited only by monks. People go there to live and die as monks; they have no other purpose in the world: their only thought is to live in the spirit of Christ's commandments. What they want is to achieve the salvation of their souls. You all know the great book of Abbot Dorotheus in which he narrates the life of his disciple Dositheus. When the Superior asks him why he has come, the disciple answers, "I am seeking the salvation of my soul." This is a classic formula among the Athonite monks.

This search for salvation appears to the monks in the following manner: All of us, just like Saint Paul, have our "road to Damascus." At a certain moment, the Lord chooses to appear to a person. This personal meeting with Christ presents the question: "If the Lord is alive here and now, how does it affect me?" There are various responses, but for some the problem is reduced to this: "If the Lord is really living and is so close to me, there is nothing for me to do but leave everything and go and sit at his feet." Now, precisely at this moment, the Holy Spirit makes us feel how unworthy we are to do such a thing. The Holy Spirit reveals our sinful state to us. We know by experience that we cannot see our sin without the light of the Holy Spirit; but when the Spirit reveals it to us, the desire for repentance is aroused in us. And we see in the Gospel how the coming of the Son of

Man, Christ, his suffering, his words, have but one end in view: to lead us to the grace of repentance.

When we begin to repent, everything changes in a way I always call "organic," or natural. There occurs the break with the rest of the world, with the people who do not feel the need to repent, who organize their life in another way. I become incapable of staying with them and sharing the course of their life. Thus Christ separates me from the world not because I naturally bear this spirit of separation within myself but because he makes me feel the need in my mind and heart of not being separated from him, and this need begins to dominate my whole life, separating me wherever I go and everywhere making me one apart, and I become a monk, that is, alone: *monachos, monos,* alone. I become alone in the way a dying man becomes alone at a certain moment despite the presence of other people.

The monk is a man who feels himself completely cut off from others, completely deprived of personal activity, a small being cast by a great love into the depths. He becomes so sensitive, so conscious of his need, that he begins to cry to God with his whole being: "Have mercy on me; *eleison!*" and this remains the leitmotiv of his whole life.

The monks of Mount Athos have no other object in life. In fact they perform no active ministry, not even in the Athonite monasteries themselves. They are obedient. For them, obedience becomes a haven of refuge in the world, because by obedience the monk obtains the royal privilege of great freedom in this world. For my mind and heart to be always free and ready for prayer, I am very much in need of a Father and of living in the spirit of obedience.

I am not going to elaborate all this for you as a scholar or theologian would; I speak to you as a simple monk. For, in reality, we are not looking for words, but to be found in God. It matters little whether I am capable or completely incapable of expressing to others what it means to be found in God. Perhaps my incapacity makes me less fit to serve others in the matter; but personally, so far as I am concerned, I am deprived of nothing. If I am in God, I have all I need and more besides.

The day on which I was ordained a Spiritual Father was a terrible one for me. Formerly, I enjoyed such liberty of spirit that I had no idea where I was or what I was doing. But, from the time that I had to share my life with others, when I had to enter into their lives, I suffered a setback.

By prayer and obedience we easily draw close to God. The monastic life sets us on a road that presents no obstacles to our union with God, although our own passions remain with us. But if I have confidence in the word of my Spiritual Father, my passions are practically removed.

I once knew a postulant who had lived in this way for five years when his superior gave him a piece of intellectual work to do. He went to his cell to do what the superior had commanded, sat down at his desk, and then experienced a strange sensation, which he later described to me. He had the distinct impression that his mind rose up out of his heart, was transferred to his brain, and only then began to examine the matter at hand. At that moment he realized that for five or six years his intellect had never separated from his heart. By this experience, which I would call negative, he understood the gift that God had bestowed on him. And I think there are many monks, everywhere, whether in the East or the West, who live like this monk in the love of Christ and in fear, a great fear — even dread, for it is a dreadful things to be separated from him.

One reads the Gospel not for others but exclusively for oneself. And when I read the Gospel I am isolated by the Word of Christ. Certain of the Fathers say that the monk eventually comes to think that "only God and I exist in the world." He forgets everything and lives without introspection, almost without thoughts, certainly without plans. You might say that his soul is cast into a great abyss. Sometimes he becomes aware of the awful distance that separates him from God, and his prayer grows more zealous in the search for Christ. This experience of being separated from God is so strong, so painful, that as a result of this pain of separation, he really forgets everything else and sometimes becomes insensible of the material world around him. But all this happens unexpectedly, with no reflection on his part, without preparation. Only afterward does he realize that it has happened. If this forgetfulness of the world is given in the form of a consolation of love, when he returns to himself he regrets his separation from God even more.

This little sketch I have given you is a résumé of our whole life.

There is nothing else to add. Everything else, all the libraries of the world, filled by all the world's wise men, even if they have been inspired by the Holy Spirit, contribute nothing further to our life.

And yet, strangely enough, this void, this liberty of spirit, this absence of all reflection, does not deprive the monk of the capacity to make judgments and to speak when the occasion requires it. He must retain such equilibrium that when others have fallen he is still standing; but experience shows that there are many people, even otherwise remarkable ones, who cannot bear this tension, who are broken by it, lose their sense of balance, and sometimes become really ill. I think that that can happen only if a monk remains attached to his own desires, defends his own way of life and his own will, if he fails in obedience, if he seeks anything at all that this world has to offer. But if none of this is so, then he feels no bad effects of this tension, which lasts, one can say, day and night, all the time. Then this tension is no longer tension, but repose. And prayer is no longer an effort, but is like a powerful stream that floods the monk's whole being, or like the air around us and within us, only more so.

On Mount Athos the monks care very little about studies. This is perhaps one of the features of Athonite monasteries that makes it so different from that of the West. Here, the monks are free of material cares, and so can devote their time to the study of theology, history, Sacred Scripture. It might be said of the Eastern monks that by comparison they are barbarians, ignorant, unlettered. Most of the monks coming to me for advice whom I have questioned on this subject have answered this way: "What do you expect of me? I am full of many passions; how can I contemplate divine things? Why should I become a theologian under my circumstances? I see no point in it."

When I asked why they were not engaged in any external ministry, their answer was: "What is there that I can do? How could I teach others without first having practiced myself the word, the commandments of Christ?" This is in accordance with the teaching of the holy Fathers, who forbade anyone to make another do something he had not first done himself; you cannot impose something on another if you have not first tried and practiced it yourself.

If we talk about the spiritual life, we should never go beyond the limits of our own experience. If I quote the Creed without living its essential message, then the Creed remains somehow exterior to me. If I read the Letters of the Apostles and they do not become my own word, my own language, the reflection of my own life, I am simply subject to an external authority. I have to live the Divine Word in such a way that it becomes my own, in the way that children absorb their mother's speech and make it their own.

I tell you this to illustrate the state of mind that keeps a monk removed from exterior activity his whole life long. And no one who is inflamed with this desire for repentance grows weary of it. He can stay that way for years and years, for his whole life, without being tired or bored. Boredom or *acedia* should never overcome our spirit.

One of you asked me if on Mount Athos the hermits always begin in cenobitic communities or if there are cases of novices going directly to a hermit. As a general rule on Mount Athos everyone who comes stays in the place where his spirit finds rest and joy. It may be in a cell in a cenobitic house, or in a small eremitical community, or with a single hermit. So there are novices who begin to live with a hermit right away. This is known as "obedience as the postulant of a hermit." But there is no system for any monk's education. Everything develops in a natural, organic way, with the passage of years, through a common life, through penance and obedience, through Holy Communion, by incessant reading of Sacred Scripture, especially the New Testament, but the Old Testament as well. The Fathers are musts to read too. Since the idea is to acquire the habit of prayer, live the life of prayer, we read about prayer. Anything else which might excite the intellect and hamper detachment of the mind and heart is avoided. For this reason there is little study of speculative theology, and theology manuals are rarely used. Theology is absorbed through the liturgical texts, which are full of dogmatic teaching; it is absorbed by the writings of the Fathers treating the problem of prayer. Since the act of prayer is the deepest and most difficult and most essential act of the monk, it naturally comes before all theological speculations for us, and as a question of life it has a different solution from that which speculative theology can offer.

On Mount Athos there is no distinction of religious orders. In the West you have Benedictines, Carthusians, Jesuits, and it is not easy to change from one order to another. On Mount Athos, and in Eastern monasticism in general, it is not so difficult to pass from one community to another. However, it is very difficult to change from the cenobitic to the eremitical life, and for special reasons. The superiors and brethren of a cenobitic monastery are very reluctant to allow a brother to become a hermit until they are sure of his motives. If someone wants to be a hermit solely because he thinks it is a higher kind of life than that of the cenobium, then he gets his wings clipped. Such a person would never become a real hermit and would risk the loss of his soul, because he thinks he is better than others.

In a providential way, and yet completely in accord with human psychology, everyone resists the man who wants to become a hermit. If a layman comes to Mount Athos and confides himself to a hermit, then there is no problem. But if a cenobite wants to become a hermit, he meets a great deal of opposition. But I think Divine Providence does him much good in this way, for one becomes a hermit only if he really needs to. There is no need to invent extravagant forms of asceticism; the eremitical vocation aims exclusively at living in the spirit of Christ's commands. It has no other idea, no other end in view. No monk should be concerned with comparing various ways of life to find out which one is the highest. Actually, the way that is higher than any other is the one to which each monk is called by the voice of Divine Providence, by the will of God. Comparisons therefore need never exist.

I beg your pardon, Fathers, for this unprepared conference. I realize that I have no gift of words, and I do not know if I have said the proper things. But I am happy and truly full of gratitude to the Lord, who has brought me into contact with you. Pray for me.

Mount Athos in Boston

Archimandrite Panteleimon

As we drove along the entrance road to Holy Transfiguration Monastery, it seemed we were leaving Boston behind, not by feet and yards but by miles. We passed a scattered grove of conifers and a small vineyard and drove over a stone bridge before sweeping up to the large red brick building. The full oddity of this solid massive structure is not immediately perceptible. It had been built in the 1880s by a rather eccentric gentleman of means who had a certain fixation on time. The building boasts one large cellar, seven entryways, twelve chimneys, fifty-two rooms, and three hundred and sixty-five windows. Off to the left is a very large carriage shed; behind, a park, a woods, a lake, and a vegetable garden. Yes, as one comes into this domain it is difficult to remember that one is indeed still within the Boston city limits, in walking distance of the Prudential Tower.

But such a recollection is even more difficult as one enters through the large front door. It is the sights and sounds of Mount Athos that greet one: the icons, the oil lamps (electric light seems to be excluded from the areas of worship and hospitality), the rhythmic call of the semantrons and bells, the rich polyphonic chant coming from the chapel. This home of truly majestic dignity and proportions passed from private hands first to a Catholic community of Sisters before coming to the Orthodox Brotherhood about ten years ago. The richly paneled hall and stately parlor easily breathed in the spirit of worship with the fragrance of incense as the monks began to use them for chapel and narthex. The paneled library serves some of the overflow crowd of faithful or the Sisters of the nearby monastery who frequently join the monks at worship, as well as providing the Brothers with a place to display their icons and other products for sale. The large summer room, with its many windows and solarium looking out over the gardens, can allow for the reception of a large number of guests. A magnificent life-size icon of the Baptist testifies to the fact that this is also used for baptisms.

As we arrived, I recalled my first visit to Holy Transfiguration. It must have been a half dozen years earlier. When we arrived, Great Vespers were already in progress, so I just slipped in among the Brothers and joined in the Service. At the end, when we went up to kiss the cross and Father's hands, his piercing black eyes scrutinized me. "And who are you?" "Basil." "What is your last name?" "Pennington." "I will see you after the Service." As Father disappeared behind the screen, we all settled down, most on the floor, as there is but one long bench in the chapel along the back wall and a single stall, usually occupied by the Gerontissa.* Darkness had fallen outside, and the chapel was now illuminated by the single lamp hanging before the royal doors and a candle on the stand next to the reader. A young monk was giving us an *ad lib* translation of the menology,* sparked with very dry wit. When he would pause in search of a word or phrase, some of the older monks who knew the text well would chime in. As Brother finished, a voice came from behind the screen: "But you have forgotten the *new* Saints." With that, Father Panteleimon appeared and began to speak to us about the "new Saints." The scene was certainly one that could have come out of John Cassian — the crowd of disciples sitting around on the floor, in the flickering light of a sole lamp, listening to their Elder. But I dare say the content of this evening's words was quite different from anything Saint John would have heard. For the "new Saints" were two monks killed by the Crusaders. As Father went on, there were many pointed shafts directed toward the Romans. I began to be more and more apprehensive about our meeting after the Service.

After half an hour or more, the Elder finally concluded his story of the life and death of the new Saints, holy Martyrs for Orthodoxy, and the community and guests filed out, each kissing Father's hand at the door as he left. We were ushered into the large reception room, where Father presently joined us in the dim light of a few oil lamps.

After further introductions and Father's recollection of other monks from my abbey who had visited, I began to hear for the first time a polemic I would hear repeated on many subsequent visits. Father began to bemoan the great heresy of ecumenism, the panheresy, the heresy that includes all heresies. Fellow Orthodox were reprobated even more than the Catholics for their infidelity in responding to Catholic overtures. On one of my later visits I was accompanied by a young Jewish professor from Georgetown University. It was a summer afternoon, and after None we had settled under a shade tree in the garden behind the house. After Father had gone on for about an hour on this usual opening theme, the young professor said rather quietly: "Father, I get the impression that you think everyone is a heretic but yourself." To this, Father replied: "Could be, could be."

Not undeservedly, then, Father Panteleimon does have something of an international reputation for being a "fierce zealot." He himself told us that the last time he went to visit the Holy Mountain the Iera Kinotis (the monastic government that rules the Holy Mountain) refused him the usual diamonitirion (the monastic passport) and he had to leave the next day. This is extraordinary, since in fact Father is himself a monk of the Holy Mountain, written in at Aghiou Pavlou.*

Father Panteleimon was born in Detroit in 1935. He is a young Elder. His family was among those Greeks expelled from Asia Minor. It is to his saintly grandmother, who could speak only Turkish, that Father attributes his monastic vocation, and to their saintly priest, the old, toothless Father Nicholas, who knew only enough Greek to celebrate the Services. Father tells delightful stories of their very loving and human pastor — he loved chocolates just like a little child and always radiated the freedom and joy of a child, too — and hopes to publish his life. At eighteen Father came to Boston to study at the Hellenic College and lived with Bishop Ezekiel, who later became Archbishop of Australia and now lives in retirement on the Holy Mountain. At twenty-one Father departed for the Holy Mountain and was clothed as a rhasophore at the great Russian Monastery of Saint Panteleimon. Already it was virtually in ruins, having declined from well over two thousand monks at the turn of the century to fewer than a hundred. But among them were some very saintly Elders. Few of them survive today, but old Father Seraphim, who was then a deacon in his sixties, remembers with fondness the fervent young Panteleimon. Father's fervor could not find contentment at the great Rossikon. Then he had the great blessing of being adopted by Father Joseph the Hesychast at New Skete. It was this very holy and renowned Elder who tonsured Father as a monk, and thus he was written in as a monk of Saint Paul's. When the Elder reposed, in 1959, his spiritual brother, Father Arsenias, took charge of the little brotherhood, which included Father Ephraim, today Hegumen of Philotheou; Father Haralambas, now Elder of the Kellion of Saint Nicolas; and Father Joseph the Younger, who continues at New Skete.

At that time, Father Panteleimon returned to America. After a relatively short time with the Bishop, Father embarked on the eremitical life near Haverhill, Massachusetts. In 1961 he was joined by Father Arsenias, and in 1962 by Father Isaac and Father Haralambas, and so the Brotherhood began to grow. They were forced to leave Haverhill and settled on Orchard Street in Jamaica Plain until they acquired the large estate in Brookline, not far from the Hellenic College. A Sisterhood also gathered around Father, and they continue to occupy the house on Orchard Street, coming to Holy Transfiguration for the principal Services.

The Community at Holy Transfiguration, which is now under Metropolitan Philaret, of the Russian Church outside of Russia, follows in great part the rule of the skete, with great emphasis on hesychasm and the Jesus Prayer. But there are some modifications in the typicon.* Since the Brotherhood has no monastery to go to for the feasts, they are celebrated in the style of a monastery at the skete itself. The ordinary day would see the monks returning to their cells after Vespers to pray on the rope (the prayer cord) until midnight, when they would gather for the Liturgy. Their hours of sleep are short and they are up fairly early to a morning of work. They support themselves largely by mounting icon prints and making some of the finest incense in the world in their great cellar. A few of the specially talented monks paint icons in studios at the top of the house. They have a very large mail-order business; orders for icons have to wait as long as three years.

*   *   *

As we entered the hall, I was delighted to see Father quickly making his way in our direction. The last time it was not so, for Father was then painfully hobbling about on crutches after surgery and a long stay in the hospital. I remembered how he laboriously made his way to us in the reception room, obviously suffering, yet with joy and peace radiating quietly from him. A sort of couch had been prepared, close to the fire, where he could be propped up on pillows. As he arrived there, one of the cats had already made himself quite comfortable in Father's place. He spoke to it quite lovingly, but then informed Brother Cat rather firmly: "You must give place, for I am the image." This deep theological outlook pervading the commonplace is typical of Father. In spite of his physical distress we had a memorable evening with Father as he talked on and on of the Holy Fathers. I have always been very impressed by the sharpness of Father's memory for endless colorful details, his encyclopedic knowledge, but above all, for his intimacy with the Fathers. As he speaks, one gets the impression — and it is not a mistaken one — that he has spent many hours sitting with these holy forebears, listening to them, imbibing their holy wisdom. For Father, for Orthodox commonly — for all of us, it should be — the Fathers are truly alive in the Lord. Death is not an end but a change, a repose. And when we come to their writings it is not a question of reading, but of listening — for the Fathers, alive in the Lord, speak to us today if we but approach them with an open and faithful heart.

Father was still far from well and foresaw further surgery in the spring. For the most part, he now stays in the small Skete of the Holy Apostles, which the community has recently established on the rocky coast of Maine in a spot somewhat reminiscent of the Holy Mountain. He had come to join the brothers for these days, for it was the middle of Great Lent, and the night before, they had had the full canon of Saint Andrew of Crete. Father expressed his great love for these long Services, so rich in mystic content. The night is too short for them.

I had spent four months on the Holy Mountain since my last visit, so as the usual refreshments were served — preserves and cold water — we shared reminiscences. Father brought from the cabinet the last photograph taken of Father Joseph the Hesychast, seated, surrounded by his disciples. His spiritual brother who has succeeded him as

Father, Father Arsenias, still lives, at the Kellion of Saint Nicolas. He is now ninety-four.

Father Panteleimon expressed mixed feelings about the renewal taking place on the Mountain. The traditions and spirit so faithfully preserved through the centuries, he feared, were in danger of being distorted or diluted. When a few come and enter the Brotherhood, they can easily be absorbed and gradually imbibe the spirit living there. But when whole Brotherhoods come from outside, even though they adopt the prevailing typicon and carry out the Services flawlessly, their spirit is apt to engulf the spirit of the few remaining seniors.

Father was especially distressed by the new practice of monks going out for studies at the universities. He met one monk in London who was studying Saint Maximos at King's College. Father found this very hard to understand. This is not the monk's way to grow in divine knowledge. His is to live in mystic communion with the Fathers. Father spoke of the three degrees of knowledge according to the teaching of Saint Isaac the Syrian. The first is profane knowledge, the arts and sciences learned at the university, and for the monk this is useless. If one has imbibed it before becoming a monk, all well and good. He can for the most part forget it. But for a monk to go back to the university to seek more of it is like a dog returning to his vomit. The second degree is that knowledge acquired through prayer, watching, fasting, studying the Sacred Scriptures and listening to the Fathers and Mothers. This is the learning proper to the monk. It awakens in him an ever greater desire for things divine. And finally there is *theoria*, that divinely infused knowledge, that experiential connatural love-knowledge, which only God can give. This is the goal of the monastic life.

In spite of this, Father could hardly be said to be anti-intellectual. It is not a question of shunning learning and knowledge but of single-mindedness, of purity of heart, of seeking the one thing necessary. His community has just published a very fine new translation of the Septuagint Psalter. This year they hope to publish a translation of Saint John Climacus, and next year, of the Macarian Homilies, including twenty-seven new ones not yet published. And they have long been laboring, using manuscripts in Greek, Russian, and Syriac, to prepare a complete translation of Saint Isaac the Syrian.

The Brotherhood has grown to nearly forty now — all they can crowd into the house. There are four priests and four deacons. Most are converts, many have little advanced education, although some do have a great deal. There is a fairly large turnover of novices, young men who are seeking and are given a chance to find. Father finds it best to restrict the novices to a fairly intense practice of the Jesus Prayer and reading the lives of the Saints, where they can find living models and helpful Fathers and Mothers in the Lord. The practice of Starchestvo — the daily manifestation of one's thoughts to the Elder — is also considered important.

With the Elder's heavy burden of hearing the brothers, instructing them, leading the long Services, searching deep in the Fathers, and above all, spending hours in mystic prayer, interceding for his sons, Father did not see how some of the new Hegumens on the Holy Mountain were finding time to write books and articles. Nor did he see the need, for we can never exhaust the immense riches the Holy Fathers and Mothers have left us. All our effort should be to enter more and more into their spirit, especially that of Saint Isaac, who so formed Father Joseph and Father Paisios and all the greatest Spiritual Fathers of our times.

The hour was growing late, and soon it would be time for Great Compline. Father took us up to the top of the house to the icon studios to see the work in process. He then presented me with copies of an icon of Saint Paul by Paniseolos. He remarked that it was an icon for monks. The long, deeply furrowed face and the wide, almost wild eyes of the mystic who saw the third Heaven have little appeal for the average faithful. This is Father's favorite icon, but of the thousands of copies he has had printed, hardly one has been sold. He commented, "Such works of faith must yet be done." I was happy to receive copies for all my brothers at home and to send to our friends on the Holy Mountain.

As we passed the great semantron on the stairs, Father paused to tell us how the little one is the voice of Noah (traditionally, he used a semantron to call the animals into the ark), the large one, the voice of the Prophets, and the metal ones, the voices of the Apostles. There is this wonderful blending in the Spiritual Fathers: the childlike simplicity in their faith alongside an immense erudition and a profoundly wise prudence in guiding souls and conducting the affairs of the monastery. We descended to the hall to venerate the life-sized icon of Saints Peter and Paul that Paniseolos did in 1956 and that Father had just brought from Greece.

By this time, the "voice of Noah" was being heard and the Brothers were making the prostrations in preparation for Great Compline. We joined them in the crowded little chapel. Beside us stood a neophyte in his white robe, with cross and burning candle in his hand. He had been baptized that afternoon. As the long Service progressed, partly in English, partly in Greek, sometimes in the soft voice of a soloist, sometimes in rich polyphony led by Father, we made the many prostrations that mark the holy Lenten season. As the Service concluded, Father asked prayers for a deceased friend, and then we all filed out, one by one, kissing Father's hand and receiving his blessing. His good-by was as warm as his welcome.

In this as in other recent visits there was none of the polemics of earlier days. Father has suffered much in these recent years, and with this there has come a mellowness. His true loving heart shines through. He is surely no less Orthodox, but zealous love has been tempered in sharing his Lord's cross. The fervent flourishing Brotherhood and Sisterhood here, as well as the large Sisterhood on the Island of Agathonissi, which he visits each year and to which he sends one of his priests for the great feasts, are ample testimony to the fact that Holy Transfiguration — a bit of Mount Athos near Boston — is blessed in the fullest sense with a true Spiritual Father.

A Noble Spiritual Mother

Mother Alexandra

I had forgotten how beautiful western Pennsylvania is. I was especially enjoying the warm sunshine and the advanced signs of spring — a pleasure undoubtedly deepened by the fact that it heralded the end of what had been a long and hard winter back home in New England. I had been driving most of the day heading east after attending the annual Cistercian Studies Conference at Western Michigan University. The turnpike was half an hour behind, and my enjoyment of the pleasant country roads was beginning to be marred by a bit of apprehension. I wondered if I had lost my way. But as I rounded the turn I caught sight of the not-too-obvious sign on the left: Orthodox Monastery of the Holy Transfiguration. I turned into the narrow road, and as the few scattered houses fell behind, it began to climb. Soon I emerged on a summit that was worthy of the Monastery's title, a bit of a Tabor, with a vista in all directions out across the rolling greens, dark and light, of the Alleghenies.

I had been looking forward to this visit, having heard years ago of the almost fabled Hegumena,* Mother Alexandra, great-grand-daughter of both Czar Alexander II, the great Russian prince who freed the serfs, and of that most formidable English sovereign, Victoria Regina. Raised at the Court of Saint James, Her Royal Highness, Princess Ileana, whose father was the first King of Romania, was wed to the Hapsburg Anton of Austria in 1931 and bore him six children. But it was not this impressive royal lineage that evoked my admiration. This courageous woman, setting aside her own comfort and safety, lived out the Gospel precept and, in the terrifying days of World War II, ministered to friend and foe alike, serving as a Red Cross nurse. Her enemies, and especially the new Communist masters of her beloved country, did not miss their opportunity. The Princess, who did not ask to which army the wounded man belonged, was branded a "war criminal" for serving the enemy — binding and healing their wounds, more with the love of Christ than with bandages and medicaments, and filling their empty stomachs. A penniless exile with six dependent children was her reward, first in South America and then in the United States. And even here her enemies pursued her as best they could. But the valiant woman succeeded in helping each of her children on his or her way and was finally free to think of her own future.

Time healed things, and the Princess was again welcome at Windsor Castle if not back in Communist-dominated Romania. But in America Her Highness had discovered something. She had found not just an interest but even a great thirst for the traditional teaching on prayer that she had imbibed as a young Orthodox. She found, too, that the Romanian Church, which in its native land, even under the Communists, knew a most flourishing Sisterhood — some convents were veritable villages, with four hundred nuns and the unending chanting of the Services — in America was almost totally ignorant of this dimension of its heritage and certainly was totally bereft of any monastic presence. Princess Ileana also discovered that having an intimate knowledge of the rich tradition of her Church — this is what sustained her through the most difficult years — she had a very real ability to teach its ways of prayer and a growing desire to devote her life to this: to pray and to teach prayer — in a word, to be Spiritual Mother.

There was little to be seen on top of the mountain to call to mind the picture of an Orthodox monastery, and yet what I beheld — a couple of red cedar lodges, one bigger than the others, and incorporating an A-frame structure (which I was to discover is the church) — was not unlike the complexes that housed the first Russian Orthodox monasteries in the Northwest of the United States. I had not yet gotten the motor turned off when the large, bustling figure of Mother Dominica emerged, all smiles and welcome. I had met Mother once before at an ecumenical meeting, so it was a happy reunion. Mother had become Orthodox back in 1966 after the not unusual confused searchings of the teen-ager. She had been with Mother Alexandra since the foundation of the community, in 1968.

After Princess Ileana had decided to become a nun, with the hope of helping the American Romanian Church rediscover this dimension of its heritage, she had journeyed to France to spend two years with the famous and saintly Mother Eudoxia at Bussey. It was there she received the tonsure and the name of Alexandra, no doubt with a thought to the great-grandfather whom she reveres. On her return to America, two years later, her first monastery was no more than a trailer, and it was there that Mother Dominica joined her.

Now there were two others in the community, and they quickly appeared behind Mother Dominica. Mother Christina, a young Orthodox, had been living in the community for four years. Novice Magdalena was a convert, a widow who had just recently arrived from England.

I was soon settled in the main room of the larger building and being served the traditional refreshment: the tall cool glass of water, appreciated on this day, which had waxed warm, and the preserved sweets. While I awaited the Hegumena, I took in my surroundings, cozy and comfortable, the red cedar walls mostly covered with bookshelves, and the ample field-stone hearth. The collection of books showed breadth and an ecumenical spirit. There were the solid basic works of spirituality, Scripture study, and patristics; such Catholic authors as Jungmann and Bouyer; the Fundamental Charismatic, Brother Andrew; Americana such as *Bury My Heart at Wounded Knee*; and various types of light reading.

It doesn't take a second look, when Mother Alexandra enters a room, to realize you are in a presence. Nobility is here, no doubt about that. And the severe, chaste robes of the Orthodox abbess add to that. But there is also a very attractive simplicity and obvious humility in this figure, and above all a radiant serenity. Suffering has made its furrows in the royal face, but love and gentleness have filled them. Mother Alexandra may be every bit a queen, but she is even more a mother.

As I enjoyed my refreshments we chatted lightly. I tried to draw out a bit of her fascinating history, but as one might have expected, she was not inclined to speak much of herself. If the talk was to be in a personal vein she would much prefer, like any grandmother, to speak of the tribe of young ones now in Detroit. She did admit that the past had not been easy. The two years under Perón in Argentina, for the devout Orthodox, had been more difficult than even the four years under the Communists and the six years under the Nazis. Mother was comfortable and at home with Catholics. In accordance with the promises she had made before her marriage, she had raised her six children, as best she could, to be devout Catholics. And if there was any sorrow in regard to her grandchildren it was that they were not as devout as they might be in their Catholic faith.

But now I became aware that with the wonderful flexibility I have constantly found in Orthodox monasteries, Vespers and supper had been pushed back, awaiting my arrival. So we rose to go to the church. Quite surprisingly, the twentieth-century A-frame, when its red cedar was bathed in the warm tones coming from large amber windows, was not at all incongruous as the setting for the age-old Byzantine Service. The iconostasis, with its familiar figures, the icons new and old, the relic shrine, the flickering lamps, and the pervading incense were all quite in place.

I was invited to take the stall next to the Hegumena as Mother Dominica's sweet voice began to intone the evening Service. It moved quickly along. Some of the more difficult parts were recited or read, rather than sung. But all was done with great dignity and prayerfulness. At the conclusion of the Service, we venerated the icons and the relics and Mother shared with me the stories behind some of them. Liturgy is only occasionally celebrated in the monastery church, for there is a great shortage of priests among the Romanian Orthodox, and, of course, a priest will never celebrate twice in the same day. On Sundays the nuns descend to the city to join the congregation there for Liturgy.

It was time for supper. It took me a bit of time to put all the elements of the refectory scene together. The room, rather long and more spacious than I would have expected in such buildings, was still the warm, rustic red cedar. But the furnishings, some fine heavy pieces, might have come from one of the Princess's manors. The nuns, in their very traditional garbs, could, with the high chairs in which they sat, have come from the Middle Ages, but the meal was very twentieth-century American and quite hearty. The hungry traveler was well cared for, and reading was dispensed with so that he could also be well entertained as the Sisters regaled him with stories of their happy life together, which had as many incongruous elements as their refectory.

During the earlier years, Mother Alexandra traveled a good bit. She was much in demand as a teacher of prayer. And admittedly she was something of a novelty to the American Romanians, not so much because of her noble lineage, which many of them revered, but as a nun. For many thought of nuns as belonging only to the Roman Catholic tradition, and it was novel to find one in their own Church. The monastery did become known, funds were raised, the present site purchased, the buildings erected quite deliberately in a simple American style, and finally a thousand and more of the faithful gathered for the consecration of the church. The monastery is more and more coming to take its meaningful place — the place that monasteries have always had — among the Orthodox faithful. Last year, in spite of heavy rain and the fact that the small community had to resort to the use of tents, some two hundred of the faithful climbed the holy hill to take part in the Anointing Service of the patronal feast.

While the Sisters busied themselves with the wash-up and chores, Mother Alexandra and I returned to the main room and talked a bit about spiritual formation. Mother was not finding it easy here. In the Romania she knew as a young woman, home life was not that different from life in the nunnery. The young ladies who came were already thoroughly familiar with the practices of the Church. They knew the Services and the Liturgy. Prayer and fasting were part of the life they had always known. Not so in America. The candidates who come have much good will but little knowledge and experience, coming from homes that knew little or nothing of Orthodox life and culture. Like most young Americans today, the young ladies are little inclined to read and have known only very abbreviated church Services. And so there is much, very much, to be done by way of formation.

The newcomer tends to want to fill the hours with doing and to keep busy with womanly homemaking tasks and chatting. Gradually they have to be led into deeper silence and won over to spending more

and more time in their cells in prayer and reading. They really have to
be taught how to read and how to pray.

Mother teaches them the way of the Jesus Prayer. Her instruction
is of the simplest sort, very personal and very practical, as she had
learned it herself decades ago at the Monastery of Sâmbata and has
practiced it through the years. There is a warm and womanly note in
her instruction:

> When you are with someone you love, when you embrace him, you
> do not stop to reflect on how or why you love, or what you are doing;
> you just love and whisper his name as love draws you. That's all
> there is to it. Be quiet. Enter into the silence of love. Repeat the
> prayer quietly, unhurriedly, thoughtfully. Every thought is focused
> on Jesus. Everything else, however good, is left to drift away. The
> Prayer simplifies. We simply repeat the Name of the Beloved.
>
> This does not happen immediately. Nothing is instantaneous. Of-
> ten, there is a long period of preparation in God's plan. We see this
> in the lives of the great Fathers, as in the Startzy such as Macarios of
> Optino.
>
> Yet even for us beginners the Jesus Prayer is a great help when we
> perceive ourselves getting bothered or taken up with many things.
> We can just sit down, put our hands in our lap, and say the Prayer
> very slowly two or three times. And then just be quiet for a time. All
> quiets down. Then we can thank and praise God and go on about
> our work with him in quiet prayer.
>
> And when it is time for us to take our rest, especially if we are
> troubled or unquiet, we can turn to the Prayer. We fall into slumber
> with it on our lips and awake with peace, and the Prayer still there.

Mother admitted that over the years she had known many an
evening when she approached her bed with a troubled spirit. Being a
Spiritual Mother is not an easy task. Over twenty-five have come to
join the community during the past decade. Each made her great
demand on Mother's love, care, and concern, and then left — all
except Dominica, Christina, and now, it is to be hoped, Magdalena.
Mother has long sought to get one or two experienced nuns from

Romania to help in her task. The nuns are willing enough to come, but the obstacles are many, seemingly insurmountable. But Mother has not given up hope.

The Sisters joined us and we spoke for a while of Mount Athos, which I had recently visited. The way of the Jesus Prayer which Mother was teaching her spiritual daughters would have come to Romania and to her from the Holy Mountain. All Orthodox look to that sanctuary of monks as the heart of Orthodoxy, and the Sisters know that on its summit, just as on the summit of their own holy mountain, there stands a chapel dedicated to the commemoration of the Holy Transfiguration of our Lord and Savior, Jesus Christ.

The hour had become late, and I had to leave early in the morning, even before the nuns would rise. Because the community is small, the Hegumena on in years, and the rest young in the monastic life, they do not keep the longer vigils. And on the morrow the Orthros would be late as we were late in bed.

Sister Dominica showed me to the guestroom adjacent to the refectory. As I looked about, taking in the modest but comfortable furnishings, I noted the two hangings that adorned the walls. They seemed to bespeak the whole vital tension that was present at Holy Transfiguration and that was the essential burden of the Spiritual Mother. One was a beautiful old icon of the Crucifixion — expressing the mystery of the Cross, of life out of death, and the rich tradition of the Christian East that brought it to this holy house. The other was an oldish American print with an inscription from *Three Men in a Boat* (1887):

> *Let your boat of life be light,*
> *   packed only with your needs —*
>
> *A homely home and simple pleasures,*
> *   One or two friends, worth the name,*
> *   Someone to love and someone to love you,*
>
> *A cat, a dog, and a pipe or two,*
>
> *And enough to eat,*
>
> *And a little more than enough to drink*
> *— for thirst is a dangerous thing.*

The first lines are good monastic advice; the description of "needs" is more debatable — especially the last. If anything, a monk needs thirst — thirst for God — and that is precisely why he deprives himself of much that others count to be needs, much of the homely and simple pleasures. But only the giants can do without them all. Every cenobium seeks to find its own blending and balance. At Holy Transfiguration, a beautiful and noble (in more ways than one) Spiritual Mother seeks to bring the Mystery of the Cross and a rich spiritual tradition to simple, pleasure-loving American women in a way that will not overwhelm or crush but, rather, gently call them forth to go beyond themselves and enter fully into the divinizing way of the Transfigured Christ.

As I drove away, down the hill, in the early dawn (after hardly doing justice to the immense spread the Sisters had laid out for my breakfast), I felt a certain joy and gratitude. The time had been short, the words few, but I had been in a Presence, one that had reached in and touched a deep place in my own heart. I thought of other Spiritual Mothers: of our own tradition, Mother Angela of Wrentham, Mère Marie de la Trinité of Les Gardes, Madre Christiana of Vitorchiano; and of the Orthodox tradition, Mother Nicodime of Ormilia; and I thanked God that his Church is blessed with Spiritual Mothers as well as Spiritual Fathers.

CONFERENCE
OF MOTHER ALEXANDRA

Lord Jesus Christ, Son of God,
have mercy upon me, a sinner

I had often read the Jesus Prayer in prayer books and heard of it in church, but my attention was drawn to it first many years ago in Romania. There, in the small Monastery of Sâmbata, tucked away at the foot of the Carphathians in the heart of the deep forest, I met a monk who practiced the "Prayer of the Heart." Profound peace and silence reigned at Sâmbata in those days; it was a place of rest and strength — I pray God it still is.

I have wandered far since I last saw Sâmbata, and all the while the Jesus Prayer lay as a precious gift buried in my heart. It remained inactive until I read *The Way of a Pilgrim.* Since then I have been seeking to practice it continually. At times I lapse; nonetheless, the Prayer has opened unbelievable vistas within my heart and soul.

The Jesus Prayer, or the Prayer of the Heart, centers on the Holy Name itself. It may be said in its entirety: "Lord Jesus Christ, Son of God, have mercy upon me, a sinner"; it may be changed to "us sinners" or it may be shortened. The power lies in the name of Jesus; thus "Jesus," alone, may fulfill the whole need of the one who prays.

The Prayer goes back to the New Testament and has had a long, traditional use. This method of contemplation based upon the Holy Name is attributed to Saint Symeon, the New Theologian (949-1022). When he was fourteen years old, Saint Symeon had a vision of heavenly light in which he seemed to be separated from his body. Amazed and overcome with an overpowering joy, he felt a consuming humility, and cried out, borrowing the publican's prayer from Luke 18:13, "Lord Jesus, have mercy upon me." Long after the vision had disappeared, the great joy returned to Saint Symeon each time he repeated the Prayer, and he taught his disciples to worship likewise. The Prayer evolved into its expanded form: "Lord Jesus Christ, Son of God, have mercy upon me, a sinner." In this guise it has come down to us from generation to generation of pious monks, nuns and laypersons.

The invocation of the Holy Name is not peculiar to the Orthodox Church but is used by Roman Catholics, Anglicans, and Protestants, though to a lesser degree. On Mount Sinai and Athos the monks worked out a whole system of contemplation based upon this simple prayer, practiced in complete silence. These monks came to be known as hesychasts.

Saint Gregory Palamas (1296-1359), the last of the great Church Fathers, became *the* exponent of the hesychasts. He won, after a long-drawn-out battle, an irrefutable place for the Jesus Prayer and the hesychasts within the Church. In the eighteenth century, when czardom hampered monasticism in Russia and the Turks crushed Orthodoxy in Greece, the Neamtzu monastery in Moldavia (Romania) became one of the great centers for the Jesus Prayer.

The Prayer is held to be so outstandingly spiritual because it is focused wholly on Jesus; all thoughts, striving, hope, faith, and love are outpoured in devotion to God the Son. It fulfills two basic injunctions of the New Testament. In one, Jesus said: "I say unto you, whatsoever you shall ask the Father in my name, he will give you. Hitherto you have asked nothing in my name: ask and you shall receive, that your joy may be full" (Jn 16:23, 24). In the other precept, we find Saint Paul's injunction to pray without ceasing (1 Th 5:17). Further, it follows Jesus' instructions on how to pray (which he gave at the same time he taught his followers the Lord's Prayer): "When you pray, enter into your room, and when you have shut your door, pray to your Father in secret, and your Father, who sees in secret, will reward you openly" (Mt 6:6).

Jesus taught that all impetus, good and bad, originates in our hearts. "A good man out of the good treasure of his heart brings forth that which is good; and an evil man out of the evil treasure of his heart brings forth that which is evil; for out of the abundance of the heart his mouth speaks" (Lk 6:45).

Upon these and many other precepts of the New Testament as well as the Old, the Holy Fathers, even before Saint Symeon, based their fervent and simple prayer. They developed a method of contemplation in which unceasing prayer became as natural as breathing, following the rhythmic cadence of the heartbeat.

All roads that lead to God are beset with pitfalls, because the enemy (Satan) ever lies in wait to trip us up. He naturally attacks most assiduously when we are bent on finding our way to salvation, for that is what he most strives to hinder. In mystical prayer the temptations we encounter exceed all others in danger; because our thoughts are on a higher level, the allurements are proportionally subtler. Someone has said that "mysticism started in mist and ended in schism." This cynical remark, spoken by an unbeliever, has a certain truth in it. Mysticism is of real spiritual value only when it is practiced with absolute sobriety.

At one time, a controversy arose concerning certain hesychasts who fell into excessive acts of piety and fasting because they lost the sense of moderation on which our Church lays so great a value. We need not dwell upon misuses of the Jesus Prayer, except to realize that all exaggerations are harmful and that we should at all times use self-restraint. Practice of the Jesus Prayer is the traditional fulfillment of the injunction of the Apostle Paul to "pray always"; it has nothing to do with the mysticism that is the heritage of pagan ancestry.

The Orthodox Church is full of deep mystic life, which it guards and encompasses with the strength of its traditional rules; thus its mystics seldom go astray. The "ascetical life" is a life in which "acquired" virtues — i.e., virtues resulting from a personal effort, only accompanied by that general grace which God grants to every good will — prevail. The "mystical life" is a life in which the gifts of the Holy Spirit are predominant over human efforts and in which "infused" virtues are predominant over "acquired" ones; the soul has become more passive than active. Let us use a classical comparison. Between the ascetic life, that is, the life in which human action predominates, and the mystical life, that is, the life in which God's action predominates, there is the same difference as between rowing a boat and sailing it; the oar is the ascetic effort, the sail is the mystical passivity that is unfurled to catch the divine wind. The Jesus Prayer is the core of mystical prayer, and it can be used by anyone, at any time. There is nothing mysterious about this (let us not confuse "mysterious" with "mystic"). We start by following the precepts and examples frequently given by our Lord. First, go aside into a quiet place: "Come apart into a desert place, and rest awhile" (Mk 6:31); "Study to be quiet" (1 Th 4:11); then pray in secret — alone and in silence.

The phrases "to pray in secret, alone and in silence" need, I feel, a little expanding. "Secret" should be understood as it is used in the Bible: for instance, Jesus tells us to do our charity secretly — not letting the left hand know what the right one does. We should not parade our devotions or boast about them. "Alone" means to separate ourselves from our immediate surroundings and disturbing influences. As a matter of fact, never are we in so much company as when we pray, ". . . seeing we also are compassed about with so great a cloud of witnesses . . ." (Heb 12:1). The witnesses are all those who pray: angels, archangels, saints, and sinners, the living and the dead. It is in prayer, especially the Jesus Prayer, that we become keenly aware of belonging to the living body of Christ. In "silence" implies that we do not speak our prayer audibly. We do not even meditate on the words; we use them only to reach beyond them to the essence itself.

In our busy lives, this is not easy; yet it can be done — we can each of us find a few minutes in which to use a Prayer consisting of only a few words, or even only one. This Prayer should be repeated quietly, unhurriedly, thoughtfully. Each thought should be concentrated on Jesus, forgetting all else, both joys and sorrows. Any stray thoughts, however good or pious, can become an obstacle.

When you embrace a dear one, you do not stop to meditate how and why you love — you just love wholeheartedly. It is the same when spiritually we grasp Jesus the Christ to our heart. If we pay heed to the depth and quality of our love, it means that we are preoccupied with our own reactions, rather than giving ourselves unreservedly to Jesus — holding nothing back. *Think* the Prayer as you breathe in and out; calm both mind and body, using as rhythm the heartbeat. Do not search for words, but go on repeating the Prayer, or Jesus' name alone, in love and adoration. That is ALL! Strange — in this little, there is more than all!

It is good to have regular hours for prayer and to retire whenever possible to the same room or place, possibly before an icon. The icon is loaded with the objective presence of the One depicted, and thus greatly assists our invocation. Orthodox monks and nuns find that to use a prayer cord helps to keep the attention fixed. Or you may find it best quietly to close your eyes — focusing them inward.

The Jesus Prayer can be used for worship and petition; as intercession, invocation, adoration, and as thanksgiving. It is a means by which we lay all that is on our hearts, both for God and man, at the feet of Jesus. It is a means of communion with God and with all those who pray. The fact that we can train our hearts to go on praying even when we sleep keeps us uninterruptedly within the community of prayer. This is no fanciful statement; many have experienced this life-giving fact. We cannot, of course, attain this continuity of prayer all at once, but it is achievable; for all that is worthwhile, we must ". . . run with patience the race that is set before us . . ." (Heb 12:1).

I had a most striking proof of uninterrupted communion with all those who pray when I lately underwent surgery. I lay long under anesthesia. "Jesus" had been my last conscious thought — and the first word on my lips as I awoke. It was marvelous beyond words to find that although I knew nothing of what was happening to my body I never lost cognizance of being prayed for and of praying myself. After such an experience one no longer wonders that there are great souls who devote their lives exclusively to prayer.

Prayer has always been of very real importance to me, and the habit formed in early childhood of morning and evening prayer has never left me; but in the practice of the Jesus Prayer I am but a beginner. I would, nonetheless, like to awaken interest in this Prayer, because, even if I have only touched the hem of a heavenly garment, I have touched it — and the joy is so great, I would share it with others. It is not every one's way of prayer; you may not find in it the same joy that I find, for your way may be quite a different one — yet equally bountiful.

In fear and joy, in loneliness and companionship, it is ever with me. Not only in the silence of daily devotions, but at all times and in all places. It transforms, for me, frowns into smiles; it beautifies, as if a film had been washed off an old picture so that the colors appear clear and bright, like nature on a warm spring day after a shower. Even despair has become attenuated and repentance has achieved its purpose.

When I arise in the morning, it starts me joyfully upon a new day. When I travel by air, land, or sea, it sings within my breast. When I stand upon a platform and face my listeners, it beats encouragement. When I gather my children around me, it murmurs a blessing. And at the end of a weary day, when I lay me down to rest, I give my heart over to Jesus: "Lord into your hands I commend my spirit." I sleep — but my heart as it beats prays on: "JESUS!"

GLOSSARY

Acathist Hymn — A Service of praise in honor of the Holy Mother of God that was composed probably in 532 and is prayed daily in Orthodox monasteries before Apodeipnon or Vespers.

Aghiou Pavlou — Saint Paul's, one of the twenty ruling monasteries on Mount Athos, situated on the southern side near the end of the peninsula.

Antidoron — When the priest prepares the bread for the Liturgy, he also prepares a tray of small pieces of bread usually from the loaf out of which he has cut the Lamb, the large square he is going to consecrate and change into the Body of Christ. Before the Communion, these pieces are brought to the altar and blessed. Those who receive Communion eat also a bit of this blessed bread, to ensure as it were that the Divine Bread is properly consumed. Those who do not receive Communion receive a bit of this blessed bread from the priest at the end of the Liturgy as a sort of lesser communion or participation in the Sacred Sacrificial Meal.

Apodeipnon — What is called in the West, Compline, the last Service of the day, celebrated at sunset.

Cenobite — A monk or nun who lives in a cenobium, q.v.

Cenobium — A monastery in which the monks live a *cenobitic* life, that form of monastic life which involves living in common obedience to a superior.

Diamonitirion — This is a permit, given by the ecclesiastical government, allowing a visitor to travel on the Holy Mountain, Mount Athos, and to seek the hospitality of the various communities.

Epitrachelion — The equivalent of the Western stole, a long, narrow vestment looped around the neck and hanging down in front, which the priest wears when fulfilling the functions of a superior.

Gerontissa — The feminine equivalent of Gerontas (Elder), the title of honor usually accorded to the Spiritual Father.

Hegumen — The head of an autonomous monastery, somewhat similar to an abbot in the West, although he need not be the Spiritual Father of the community. He is usually elected by the community.

Hegumena — The superior of a convent of nuns.

Hesychasm — A quality of stillness, or silence. This term can be interpreted at many levels: exteriorly, meaning solitude or withdrawal into a cell; interiorly, a certain return to oneself, inner silence, spiritual poverty, a listening to God.

Hesychast — One who practices or has entered into a life of hesychasm.

Hierodeacon — A deacon who is a monk.

Hieromonk — A monk who is a priest.

Hieroschimonk — A priest-monk who has received the great, or angelic, habit, which is also called the schema. The significance of this is interpreted variously in the various Orthodox traditions.

Iconostasis — A partition, usually with three openings, set between the nave and the sanctuary in Eastern Christian churches. It is covered with many icons arranged according to a set pattern.

Idiorrhythmic — A style of life, adopted in some of the monasteries of Orthodoxy in the fourteenth century due to historical circumstances and still prevailing in some, by which the monks receive an allowance from the common income, retain their property, and do not have a common superior or lead a common life.

Karoulia — A skete at the southern extremity of Mount Athos. The households of the skete are scattered over a rather considerable area of very rough terrain. Many hermitages are found in the same district. The monks of this area are known for the strictness of their life.

Katholicon — The principal church of a monastery.

Liturgy — While this term is used in the West to refer to the whole of the public worship of the Church, among the Orthodox and in this book it refers to the Eucharistic Sacrifice only.

Megaloschemos — A monk who has received the great, or angelic, habit. Originally there was only one monastic profession and one monastic habit, or schema, but in time a variation of grades developed; hence the distinction between the little and the great schema. In the Russian tradition, taking the great schema means committing oneself to a more exclusively contemplative life; in the Greek tradition this is not necessarily so, and some of the monasteries on Mount Athos do not observe the distinction but immediately give the great schema to all monks. The habit includes the robe, or tunic; leather belt; rhason (q.v.); skouphos, or hat; veil; mandyas, or cloak; and the analabos which is the proper part of the great schema. This last resembles in its form the scapular worn by Western monks but probably has no connection with it in its origins. It is of black cloth or soft leather and has embroidered on it, usually in red, the Cross of Calvary with spear, reed, and sponge; the skull of Adam; and certain monograms. It is usually worn only when the monk or nun is going to receive Holy Communion.

Menology — A book containing the lives of the saints arranged according to the order in which their feasts occur in the calendar.

Metania — Among the Orthodox, the various kinds of ceremonial reverences are distinguished as follows: a) proskynesis: bowing down and touching the ground with one hand; b) gonyklisia: going down on both hands and both knees; c) metania: there are two kinds: great, going down on hands and knees and touching the ground with the forehead, and little, a low bow of the body.

Metropolia — The Russian Orthodox Church in America, which has been recognized by the Russian Patriarch as an autocephalous church, i.e., independent of the Patriarchate and having its own head, the Metropolitan.

Monastic Republic — The semiautonomous State of the Holy Mountain, situated on the northernmost peninsula jutting out from Khalkidhiki, in northern Greece. The peninsula is dominated by the imposing Mount Athos and has been the home of monks from time immemorial. In 969 the first cenobium was established, and soon others developed to form a federation that elected a synod to rule the peninsula. Only Orthodox monks may live in this republic.

Mount Athos — The reference is to the Monastic Republic, q.v.

Orthros — One of the principal Services prayed by Orthodox, usually at dawn.

Phelonion — The large outer vestment worn by an Eastern Christian priest when he is fulfilling his more important functions. It is roughly equivalent to the chasuble in Western Christian vestiture.

Philokalia — A collection of ascetical and mystical writings from the monastic Fathers put together in five volumes by Macarios of Corinth and Saint Nikodimos of the Holy Mountain in the eighteenth century.

Prayer cord, *komvoschinion*, or *tchotki* — Used by the monks, and by lay people also, in their prayers, especially when they are praying the Jesus Prayer, not so much to keep count, although that is part of it, as to facilitate attention. It is usually made of black wool, although sometimes strands of other colors or colored beads are added for decoration. In a properly made cord each knot is very carefully and prayerfully made with much symbolism going into its construction. The usual cord has one hundred knots separated into sections of twenty-five by a bead, and having as a pendant a woven cross. A full cord, of three hundred knots, might be used in the cell, and a smaller one, of fifty, in the pocket.

Proskomidia — A ceremony performed before the celebration of the Liturgy at a table on the left side of the sanctuary, where the priest prepares the bread and wine that is to be used in the Liturgy. Part of the ceremony involves cutting small pieces of bread and placing them on the *diskos*, or plate, while asking the

Lord to remember particular intentions. In this way the priest brings the particular intentions of the faithful to the Liturgy.

Protaton — The oldest church on the Holy Mountain, having served the Synod and its predecessor, the original Synaxis, for nearly ten centuries. It is situated at the very center of the capital. The frescoes that cover the walls of the Protaton were painted in the fourteenth century by a celebrated artist from Thessaloniki, Panselinos.

Rhason, also called the Mandorrhason or Pallium — An outer garment, reaching to the ankles and having wide sleeves, which is worn by the married clergy as well as the monks. For the monks and for Greek clergy it is always black, but the Russians wear various colors. Its origins are traced back to the garment worn by Turkish officials in court in the high Middle Ages.

Rhasophore — A novice who has received the rhason but has not made the vows. The extent to which he is really a monk is interpreted variously by various traditions. Most monasteries on Mount Athos do not have rhasophores but immediately admit novices to full monastic profession.

Rossikon — A popular name for the Russian monastery on Mount Athos: Aghios Panteleimonos, or Saint Panteleimon's.

Semantron — A board, usually about eight feet long and six to ten inches wide, that a monk carries about the monastery, striking it with a wooden mallet to announce the Services. A very particular rhythmic stroke is employed which engraves itself in the memory of any visitor. Tradition says this is the way Noah called the animals into the ark. There are larger semantrons of wood and smaller ones of metal hung in place, usually near the entrance of the katholicon, which are also used.

Skete — Usually a very small household, of two or three to six or more monks (today it sometimes means only one), or a cluster of such households. Historically there have been some very large sketes, monasteries remaining in dependence on a large, autonomous monastery.

Skhimnik or skhimonk — A monk who has received the great schema, see Megaloschemos.

Starchestvo — A practice whereby the monk reveals to his Spiritual Father all his inner thoughts, intentions, and temptations, and receives his counsel. It is usually done daily, at least at the beginning of monastic life, and is a most effective means to move toward inner quiet and purity of heart.

Staretz, pl. Startzy — The Russian word for "Spiritual Father."

Stavrophore — A monk who has the little habit; see Megaloschemos.

Tonsure — The word most commonly used by Orthodox to speak of the monastic profession. The profession ceremony includes three elements: making the vows or promises in response to questions placed by the Hegumen, having one's hair ritually cut (tonsure), and receiving the monastic habit.

Typicon — The rule of a particular monastery which spells out the details of the daily life and especially the way in which the Services will be conducted.

Valaam — An Orthodox monastery, now suppressed, situated on an island in Lake Ladoga, in northern Russia.

Praise to you, Lord Jesus Christ, Savior.